One of a Kind

One of a Kind

Essays in Tribute to Gustave Weigel

WITH AN INTRODUCTION BY
REV. JOHN COURTNEY MURRAY, S.J.

Dimension Books
WILKES-BARRE, PA.

THE CONTRIBUTORS

FATHER JOHN COURTNEY MURRAY is the nation's most distinguished Catholic Theologian. A fellow Jesuit and close friend of Father Weigel, Father Murray has also been a pioneer in the ecumenical movement.

JUAN OCHAGAVIA, S.J., was a former student of Father Weigel in Chile.

DR. ALBERT C. OUTLER is Professor of Theology at Southern Methodist University and author of *A Christian Context for Counseling.*

DR. DOUGLAS HORTON is a Congregational minister, former Dean of Harvard Divinity School and the author of numerous books, among them *Out Into Life.*

REVEREND JOHN B. SHEERIN, C.S.P. is Editor of *The Catholic World.* He was a good friend of Father Weigel and worked with him in the earliest American Catholic efforts at ecumenism.

REVEREND HOLT M. JENKINS is an Episcopal priest, pastor of All Saints' Church in Atlantic City, New Jersey.

FATHER EUGENE BURKE, C.S.P., is a member of the Department of Theology at both Catholic University and Trinity College.

ROBERT BALKAM is Chairman of The Gustave Weigel Society and Editor of its newsletter, *Convergence.*

ROBERT McAFEE BROWN, Professor of Religion at Stanford University, was co-author with Father Weigel of *An American Dialogue.*

TABLE OF CONTENTS

One of a Kind

A MEMORABLE MAN

by REV. JOHN COURTNEY MURRAY, S.J.

The tides of time run with terrible rapidity these days; once left behind, one is soon forgotten. It is therefore pleasant that friends of Fr. Gustave Weigel, at the instance of another friend, Mr. Thomas P. Coffey, should have wished to put together these memorabilia. He was a memorable man. Characteristically, he disappeared suddenly in midstream; he was no man to find an end in the shallows or backwaters.

It was in 1930, when both of us were first-year theologians at Woodstock, that my friendship began with the tall, very thin, awkward, angular young man from Buffalo, with the sloping shoulders, then erect, which were to bow with the years. It was an unlikely friendship, between two men who were in almost every respect quite different; but it grew over the years to extraordinary depths of understanding and loyalty.

One fact stands out. In the years between 1930 and 1964 he changed greatly — only to become more like himself, the man whom first I knew. Only one significant thing was added — the wry ironic sense of humor that was so characteristic of the older man. I do not remember it present in his youth. He was serious to the point of intensity, a completely dedicated student, averse to all athletics as he always remained), not inclined, as I was, to run with the "cowboy set," as it was called in the slow old days (most of the cowboys are dead now, and they have left no heirs). The wider and deeper humanity, of which the later humor was the sign, was wrought into Gus by the passing years and by the experiences which filled them, not all of which were pleasant.

During his study of philosophy he had worked extensively in Emmanuel Kant and then in Maréchal. The imprint remained. I never could fathom his epistemology or even parts of his theological thought. It might be too much to say that he was a Platonist, save in the general sense in which every man is either Platonist or Aristotelian. Surely he was what the Germans call a *Soseinsdenker,* one who constructs his world of thought in categorical terms. (It was one of the interesting contrasts in his character that in the world of community, as distinct from the world of theory, he was an uncompromising realist.) He had none of the talents of the historian — the ability and inclination to piece together an era or a man in dependence on the available evidence.

This lack was later to occasion him trouble. During our undergraduate days we had worked together on the era of the Semipelagian controversy — he on Faustus of Riez, I on the lesser figure, Prosper of Aquitaine. He chose to continue this work for his doctoral thesis in Rome. The first part of his lengthy dissertation purported to be a reconstruction of the history of the controversy. The trouble was, as his readers pointed out respectfully but firmly, that he had written the history as it ought to have been, not as it was. To the end of his life this categorical mentality perdured. History — not to say exegesis — always remained what Gus's scheme of thought required it to be. At that, the rejection of the first part of his doctoral thesis (the second, analytical part was accepted with honors) had one providential result. He had been destined for a professorship at the Gregorian University; instead he was sent to Chile — and to all the brilliance of his career there.

The strength and the independence and the confidence of his intelligence were early apparent, and these traits grew more marked with the years. His ideas were wrought out by himself, never in argument with others. In fact, in the beginning as at the end, it was almost impossible to argue with him. Even if there were agreement, he would normally state it by saying, "Let's put the matter in these terms" — his terms. If there were disagreement, that was the end. Except once. I recall that in our student days we clashed on some issue or other (I have forgotten what it was). It was one of many clashes, but this time the outcome was unique. He had argued for position A, and I for position B, far into the night. The next morning he came to my room just before I went to his. "John," he said, with wonted directness, "I've been thinking. You were right and I was wrong." It was the very thing I was about to say to him. We then began the whole argument all over again, having changed sides — and this time with the usual outcome.

Collective thought was not for him; he would have no part of it. He would sit, for instance, through a whole faculty meeting and say nothing — until afterwards, when he would tell me what he thought. The point is that he would tell me; it was not a matter of argument. This disposition to withdraw from the process of collective thinking increased according to the subject matter. Once at a conference in Cambridge which had to do with moral problems he sat for two days without a word. Finally, the chairman addressed him directly. His reply was: "I take no interest in morality." That was true — and that was the end.

This disposition to think by himself and not with others may explain why it was that in the pre-conciliar period and at the Council itself he took no part, and wanted to take no part, in the work of the sub-commissions of the Secretariat for the Promotion of Christian Unity, to which he was attached. Not for him was the bruising business of composing a text in collaboration with other minds. I chided him, for instance, for his disinclination to put an American hand to the drawing up of the two pre-conciliar texts on religious freedom. He simply remained disinclined. His work at the Council was in another area. And there is ample evidence in this volume, and in the larger memory of all the Protestant observers, of the competence and devotion with which he did it.

Our ways parted after graduate studies. He never wrote to me from Chile, nor I to him from Woodstock. But in 1949 we took up exactly where we had left off, in the confidence of a reciprocal loyalty. That was probably the most difficult year, in a spiritual sense, of his whole life. His ejection (the term is not too strong) from his adopted land, which he loved, had aspects of both substantive and procedural injustice. This has to be said now. But I never once heard him cry out. He was not the cry-baby type which has curiously appeared in the post-conciliar era. In fact it was only gradually that I learned the whole story; he was most reluctant to talk about it (not from him would the story ever have been gleaned, if in those days the *National Catholic Reporter* had existed).

At that, his difficulty was not in bidding the past goodbye; the glory of it — and there was much glory in it — meant nothing to him. His difficulty was to find himself in the present. He was at a loss — in fact, lost. A year at Woodstock as professor of cosmology and lecturer on German literature was no more than a stop-gap.

(Incidentally, speaking of his German, I recall some mutual German friends at the Council saying how "quaint" it was. He spoke the language with fluency, but apparently he never lost the Alsatian accent and twist of idiom that he had picked up at home as a child. I might add that to have known the father and mother, as I did slightly, was to understand the son. The father was a grave gentleman of great dignity; the mother was a peasant woman full of warmth and kindness. Often I teased Gus about the peasant quality in him; he always gloried in it. I remember too his grief when his mother died while we were in Rome; he wept.)

In 1949 he was stripped of all distinction; he was no longer a name. And he needed to be a name, not out of personal vanity, of which he was devoid, but simply because he was himself, conscious and confident of his powers. Fortunately, I was able to point to one way out of the void. *Theological Studies* had been looking for a specialist in Protestant theology. He plunged into the area with mounting zest. The first results were two articles in the 1950 volume of *Theological Studies*, "Contemporary Protestantism and Paul Tillich," and "Protestant Theological Positions Today." With something less than fifty pages he made a name for himself. The further result was his ensuing career as a pioneer in ecumenism. In the summer of 1950 I attended the founding meeting of the Catholic Ecumenical Conference at the marvelous Greek-Latin Basilian abbey in Grottaferrata. Most of the meeting was given over to reports from various countries on the state of ecumenical affairs. In my turn I had to report that there was no ecumenical activity in the United States, and that no one wanted any, least of all the Catholic bishops. That was the situation into which Gus strode with all his force of intelligence and sympathy of spirit. He, more than anyone else, initiated the change.

At the same time he threw himself into his new work as professor of ecclesiology. He wrote his own treatise on the Church (it came to be known to his students as the Golden Book, by reason of his yellow covers). As a work of theology it would not do today, but in its moment it was what the French call a "réalisation," a highly personal synthesis—with, I must say, a few Platonist overtones marked by those who affectionately referred to "Gus's Church," in contrast to the real Church which functioned in the parish at the foot of the Woodstock hill.

In this moment of ongoing activity he was struck down. For nearly three months he lingered in the valley of the shadow of death, and there were longer months of slow convalescence. I should prefer to draw a veil over the whole painful episode — a major operation, a pulmonary congestion, a renal failure, an intestinal obstruction, a second major operation, a lengthy healing, a final surgical procedure. The light that shone from out the shadow was his own immensely

17

fearless fortitude; ask a nurse, for instance, to tell of a patient who for weeks never once flinched from a single one of countless "needles," not to speak of greater agonies. This claims a place among the memorabilia.

But there is something else which is harder to describe. The night before his first surgery he was quiet and serene, free of all apprehension. But I also came away with the strange impression that he did not want to live and did not intend to. He later corroborated the impression; but he never explained his sense of having reached the end. In some psychological sense it was a reaction to what he — a strong man who had never been ill — considered an aggression and an injury. In the deepest sense I think it was a resignation — to the point, as it were, of a capitulation — to the will of God. An instinct for the will of God was the cornerstone of his spirituality, on which was erected an edifice of striking simplicity and enormous solidity. But for once he had forgotten the hypothesis.

The aftermath had its amusing aspects. With wonted irony and no less wonted affection he used to blame me for having brought him back. He liked to recall what may have been true — that I once said to him: "Gus, if you die on me now, I'll never speak to you again." He even remembered how, in a moment when he had all but gone his way, I had shouted at him in German (oddly, only in his earliest familial language was it then possible to get through to him at all). The wry detached humor never left him even in the worst moments. Fr. Joseph Murphy, the Rector of Woodstock (whose devotion to Gus during those months was endless) and I were once summoned in the middle of the night, to find a dozen doctors and nurses laboring over him. Almost unconscious, he caught sight of us and growled with gasping breath, "It was hardly necessary to call out the Marines."

This spiritual aspect, so to speak, of his illness needs to be understood in order to understand the ten years that were left to him. He had a sense of living on borrowed time. It made a subtle difference. I might state the difference quite simply — perhaps too simply — by saying that he more and more abandoned the world of theory, which had been his first love, and went over more and more completely to the world of community, in which his final achievements were to be wrought. He went back to the classroom; he read and wrote. But for the most part he lived on his accumulated intellectual capital, which was considerable. For instance, he came soon to realize that the Golden Book was out of date, but he never brought himself to revise it. He was aware, of course, of ongoing trends in ecclesiology; his last lecture before he died was on the notion of the pilgrim Church. But the enterprise of scholarship as such was somehow beyond him, or behind him. He put himself increasingly at the service of others, to do what anybody asked him to do.

The motivation was complex, as human motivations always are. Part of it was his sense of the will of God, which for him was concretized in the task at his elbow, in the call that came from someone. Part of it was related, in some way I cannot explain, to a sense that his own life, lived under the impulse of inner dynamisms, had come to an end. Now the dynamism had to be exterior, in the form of demands made on him from without. The demands were many and they multiplied in the last years. Invitations to speak poured in on him, and he accepted them whenever plane or train schedules made it possible. He met his classes faithfully, but more often than not without preparation. I used to remonstrate with him and protest his lack of discrimination; he spoke on many important occasions but also on trivial ones. But he was unwilling to discriminate; each invitation was a call from someone — and that was enough for him. Did he enjoy it all? I think not. But the question itself was irrelevant. His fundamental disposition came out in a remark that he often made when confronted with something he did not want to do but had promised to do: "I've married the witch of Endor; I'll be faithful to the witch of Endor."

I saw little of him except in passing, during the second session of the Council when we were in Rome together. We lived apart and were differently engaged. Tributes to his work have been recorded with great sensitivity by those who were its immediate beneficiaries, the Protestant observers. I need add nothing to the tributes, though I must express my own gratitude for them. One morning as the second session was drawing to its rather dismal close I encountered Gus in the Basilica. He said: "John, I shall not come back for the next session." I do not know whether he was being consciously prophetic; at the time I thought he was speaking out of exhaustion and out of a concomitant depression, which most of us shared. Perhaps he knew that he bore his death within him?

At any rate, it showed up on a chest x-ray that he was prevailed upon to have taken by a distinguished radiologist at the Johns Hopkins Hospital, a week before his death. The technical details do not matter; they had to do with an advanced arteriosclerotic condition of the aorta (as well as I remember). The condition argued the possibility of instant death from a dissecting aneurism, at a moment that was unpredictable. The doctor was a close personal friend who knew Gus and his temperament; therefore with wisdom and tact he did not disclose the seriousness of the condition. There was nothing to be done about it, and Gus himself was not likely to do anything — or rather, to stop doing any of the things to which he had committed himself. I saw him that same evening, asked him the results, and was told that all was well. In the offhand way that we affected between us I said: "Please don't think you are out of the woods." He answered: "I never was in the woods." They were the last words we exchanged. He was not a man of the darkling woods, the *selva oscura*. He was "light in the Lord" (Ephesians 5:7), lightsome within his own being and a light for the community around him.

THE GRINGO

by JUAN OCHAGAVIA, S.J.

Seated among the delegates of the Orthodox and Protestant churches inside the Renaissance nave of St. Peter's basilica during the sessions of Vatican II, a Jesuit priest could be seen every day completely absorbed in explaining to those about him the meaning and scope of the themes under discussion. He was Fr. Gustave Weigel. Personally, I had known him since my school days in Santiago, Chile. I recall the impression that the sudden appearance of this "gringo" in the patio of the College of St. Ignatius summoned forth — tall and disheveled, making incredible efforts to make himself understood in a rudimentary Spanish. It was the spring of 1937.

Twenty-six years had succeeded in bending his shoulders and in adding, as well, a pronounced tired look to his eyes; for his 57 years he seemed to have aged prematurely. For the rest, the appearance of the Jesuit seated in the observers' tribune at the Council corresponded perfectly to the image which I had preserved from my childhood: his broad, intelligent forehead, his smile capable of expressing the whole gamut of feelings from a frank and cordial welcome to an expression of irony or displeasure.

These twenty-six years had made of Father Weigel one of the most beloved and respected personalities in the movement of church renewal, as much in Chile as in the United States. Of this we were sure, and the number of those among us who considered themselves his friends or had benefited from his services defied reckoning. This was also most apparent to me when I arrived in the United States in 1954, six years after this Gringo, so beloved by the Chileans, had returned to his country for the last time. All one had to say in the United States was that he came from Chile, and people from the most diverse walks of life would immediately ask, "Then you know Father Weigel?" And the very tone of the question gave clear proof of admiration and affection and a certain pride of being counted among those who knew this man, who would eventually become a symbol in the United States.

In view of this, when the cable brought word that Father Weigel had passed away in New York on January 3, 1964, of a heart attack, countless Chileans felt that we were losing one of our most loyal friends; from a Christian point of view, we were moved with a mixture of joy and sadness in knowing that the Gringo (this eventually became his name here in Chile) had gotten ahead of us on his way to God.

Family and Formation

Born in Buffalo on January 15, 1906, Gus (as he was called in North America) inherited from his parents, children of Alsatian emigrants, the dialect of his forebears and the love of the traditions of the German people. He used to say that it was in the dialect of Alsace that he learned his first words and certainly his first prayers. During one of our conversations in Rome a few weeks before his death, he alluded to his former countrymen: in certain things he considered himself very *Bauer*. This, together with the frankness and disarming simplicity of the North Americans from the Great Lakes region, made him always fundamentally candid. He avoided empty etiquette and meaningless formality. He sought after the genuine, the authentic, the meaningful, and not the more or less false ways of a certain formality or certain mannerisms of religious piety. Later on, when dealing with people he encountered face to face, he could not disguise his ill-feeling and showed it with his usual irony and sense of humor. To those who did not understand, this irony was somewhat jolting, but deep down it did them good, because it forced them to come back down to earth. The ironic candor of Father Weigel used to remind us of the ceaseless questions of Socrates — whom he admired and who brought into question the false security of the citizens of Athens — although Father Weigel had much more heart and goodness than did the old Greek philosopher.

When he had finished his years with the nuns in parochial school (on this score, he used to say, "You can study all the theology you want; but, in the last analysis, what the nuns taught you is what you are going to retain"), Gus continued on to Canisius High School, run by the Jesuits. There he distinguished himself as a debater, a trait he preserved throughout his life. Avery Dulles, S.J., a student of Father Weigel at Woodstock and later his colleague, in an account of Father Weigel written after his death, recalled "the invincible debating tactics" which he employed as a teacher. For my part, I recall that both during the time that I had him as a professor at the College of St. Ignatius and throughout my years of theology at Woodstock, the Gringo enjoyed provoking a good discussion that would awaken the dormant interests of the students and would impel them to penetrate to the depths of problems. Naturally, in these debates the quick wit and profound mind of the professor always triumphed. On one occasion only did I see him completely disarmed — with laughter. This was when a friend of mine, now a missionary in India, in an attack of Irish vehemence, mounted the rostrum and shouted at him defiantly: "Will you let me talk?"

Gus entered the Jesuit Novitiate of New York in July, 1922, after graduating from Canisius at the age of 16. Of his period of formation in the Society, he remembered with special fondness the years of philosophy and theology spent at Woodstock (1926-1929, 1930-1934). From that time, Woodstock became for him his true home. He felt a very great love for the library and the grounds. He enjoyed spending the time after lunch working in the garden and keeping the grass in the small cemetery well cut. He maintained this habit even in the most feverish activity of his last years.

One of the things Father Weigel remembered best from his years of philosophy at Woodstock was the deep and enriching friendships that grew up among the philosophers, friendships that were nourished through contact with the great problems of philosophy and the ideals of the priesthood.

During the years of theology, thanks above all to his collaboration with his companion and friend, Fr. John Courtney Murray, Gus began to realize the many shortcomings of a theological formation based on the traditional manuals, and he gave himself zealously to the study of the great authors. His reading of Fr. Maurice de la Taille's *Mysterium Fidei* had a decisive importance in his life and provoked what he used to call his "conversion" to Christianity. One night, while reading this work, he came across a quotation from St. Augustine and understood with a luminous intensity the decisive role of Christ's grace in the spiritual life of the Christian and in the unfolding of human events. Until that time, he said, he had lived a Kantian spirituality based on one's own effort and in doing things "through duty." Augustine, on the other hand, showed him the freeing force of that grace which makes us feel delight in the quest for

God, thus opening up the floodgates to love. From that moment, his love and admiration for St. Augustine grew ever more. There was, without a doubt, a notable affinity of temperament between the vehement and brilliant genius of Augustine and the great heart of Father Weigel which was open to all. Furthermore, paradoxically, though his heart was more in tune with the rhythm and fullness of the genius of Augustine, the ideal of his intellectual life became the rational and architectonically-woven thought of Thomas Aquinas. In philosophy as well as in theology, he enjoyed knowing that he was the heir of the great spiritual tradition which, beginning with biblical revelation on the one hand, and with Socrates and Plato on the other, reached its greatest consistency and fullness in St. Thomas. But he was far from that archaic "Thomism" which returns a thousand and one times to the formulae of St. Thomas as though one were going to contemplate the objects in a museum. St. Thomas was for him much more a quarry to which he would go to find inspiration to face on his own terms the problems of today. In this he always felt moved by the vital Thomism of his two confreres, the French Jesuit, Pierre Rousselot, and the Belgian, Joseph Maréchal.

Eleven Years in Chile
After his ordination to the priesthood and upon completion of his ordinary studies in the United States, Father Weigel was sent to Rome to earn a doc-

torate in theology at the Gregorian University. His enthusiasm for St. Augustine inspired him to write his doctoral thesis on Faustus of Riez, in this way obliging himself to penetrate deeply into Augustine's works on grace and on the controversies that they provoked. Having finished his work in two years, he was notified one day that from Rome he would go to Chile to assume the chair in dogma of the recently founded Faculty of Theology at the Catholic University. It was the summer of 1937 in Europe. He used to say that his first reaction was to tell the news to his friend, Fr. John Courtney Murray. Immediately they both went in search of a map to find out exactly where Chile was. This sudden appointment was not exactly to his liking, but he used to tell me that at that moment the only important thing to him was to find out if he could spend a few days in the U.S. to say goodbye to his relatives and to collect his belongings. And so it was that Father Weigel reached Santiago, and Catholic University, during our springtime.

In Chile he soon won the esteem of the clergy and of university circles for his vast store of knowledge, his profundity in theology and philosophy, and his notable common sense. Throughout his courses and conferences, he stamped his personal mark on an entire generation of our country's clergy, communicating to it his spirit, which was open to progress, realistic and hard-working. Many of the qualities that have signalized the bishops of Chile during the Council reflect the judgments and ways of seeing things that

29

Father Weigel passed on to those fortunate enough to have been his students.

But it would be presenting a false picture of reality to make Father Weigel's influence solely in the academic field. There are other factors which explain the incredible influence that he exercised on the most diverse cross-sections of our country. One of these was his total openness and availability to others. For good or for bad, he did not put great stock in movements and institutions — except in the institution of learning — but he did believe wholeheartedly in the value of friendship. Hence it was that he gave himself without reserve to people, to anyone who needed his help and who, without false formalities, sought out his friendship.

Another of these factors is perhaps best expressed in the saying that was heard so often and that made him laugh so much when it came from the mouth of a woman who was something of a snob: "This Father is so understanding . . . so human." Father Weigel was the first North American priest to establish roots in Chile. His frank and forward ways began to project an image of the priest different from the one in vogue until that time in our country. The Gringo smoked, told jokes (upon meeting him you would think that he always had some joke on his mind), and it was perfectly natural for him to think of a priest going about without a cassock. These were only small manifestations — without great worth in themselves — of something more profound which shone through during his entire life: because of his interest, because of his worries or his likes, the priest has no reason to be distant or different from the rest of men. On the contrary, the priest has to know how to immerse himself and become interested in all the dimensions of human reality in order to offer them and elevate them to God. In this sense, spiritually speaking, more is demanded of the priest: to make his the interest of humanity — not only his very own but those of all men — but maintaining at the same time an acute sense of the meaning of the divine mystery which takes place each day in his hands.

In these circumstances it is easy to understand that Father Weigel was literally swamped with petitions from people asking him for courses, conferences, articles or spiritual direction. In 1942 he had been named dean of the Faculty of Theology, but his activity greatly surpassed the office of dean and his theology classes. He gave classes in Catholic culture at the Catholic University, taught philosophy at St. Ignatius, religion at Villa Maria and in the Instituto Carrera. His room at the College of St. Ignatius came to be practically a club where problems in philosophy and religion were discussed in a cloud of smoke. It may sound strange, but very often, in order to speak with him in private, it was necessary to ask him to leave his room.

In his frequent theological conferences (the person of Christ, the Church, the Eucharist, and matrimony were favorite themes), he not only did not limit him-

31

self to exposing the doctrine but he projected it into the situations of daily life, browbeating us Chileans with ironic humor for our lack of objectivity and spirit of work, for our laziness and lack of social consciousness.

So much activity was taking its toll. The Gringo scarcely had time to sleep. He used to tell me that frequently he found himself dozing on the bus or while he was waiting for someone. He was prevented from dedicating more time to deep study and remaining abreast of theological developments. This grieved him and made him uneasy but, given the urgency of the problems with which people came to him, he did not feel justified in putting them off. What is notable is that amidst this feverish activity he should have the patience and perseverance to write out each day the text of the class, sermon or conference he was going to give, be they for his students or colleagues. Even more notable is that he should have had the time and energy to write *El Cristianismo Oriental* (1945) and *La Psicologia de la Religion* (1946), two works which are still important. He also published numerous magazine articles.

Exiled in His Own Country

At the beginning of 1948, Father Weigel made a trip to the United States. He planned to return before the new academic year at the beginning of March. While there, he received a letter from the Superior in Rome ordering him to remain in his own country.

The order was for the Gringo a tragedy which he felt
very deeply. He was completely in love with the Chileans. His priestly heart was full of anxiety, thinking
about the fate of so many friends who depended on
him for their Christian orientation. But he was deeply convinced that in God's work no one can pretend
to be indispensable. He used to repeat frequently,
"The work of God is *God's* work." He knew that
obedience — and in this the Jesuit must signalize
himself — is the road towards liberty and light. And
so he must begin to walk this path. The beginnings
were very difficult. He felt terribly tired and sleepy.
The doctor told him: "You don't need sleep. The
trouble is that you refuse to face this new reality."

But this resistance was overcome by his will to
obey. Six years later, he told me he believed that remaining in the U.S. was for him a providential act of
God. The work in Chile was draining him physically
and mentally. It was excessively fatiguing, excessively varied, prevented him from producing the things
of greater value to which he felt himself called. He recalled with a laugh his famous conferences in Santiago prepared on the run and whose themes stretched
from the most difficult theological point to a description of the flowers on the Alps. Now he felt a need
for study and reflection in order to answer the great
problems with which the present-day Church was
faced.

He imprisoned himself again in Woodstock to
study. In theology he taught the tracts on the

Church, on the act of faith, and on tradition, besides the course on the Oriental Churches which he loved so much. His love for the theological tradition of Tubingen (J. B. Mohler, K. Adam, R. Geiselmann) helped inject new life into the somewhat too scholastic atmosphere of Woodstock and to open it to present-day problems. He began a friendly dialogue with the great Protestant theologian, Paul Tillich, which can be considered a model of serene, cordial and fruitful study. He wrote various articles on the burning theme of Church and State, following the line of the controversial thesis of his friend John Courtney Murray, a thesis which — as both could witness during the Council — continues to gain more favor with theologians. In view of the controversies provoked by the encyclical *Humani Generis* (1950), he made a rich balance of the positions and planned judicious directives to advance the work of theology.

Father Weigel was very much interested in philosophy, especially metaphysics and epistemology. With the occasion of a course in cosmology, which he had to give for two years to the philosophers at Woodstock, he penetrated the epistemological problems created by American logical positivism. These studies served as the basis for the courses in metaphysics and religion which he gave each summer at Fordham University and which, in turn, appeared later on as books entitled *Knowledge* (1961) and *Religion and Knowledge of God* (1961).

The Valley of Death

Towards the end of 1953, Father Weigel went to Germany on an educational exchange mission for the State Department to give conferences at the University of Tubingen and at the University of Mainz. There he felt the first symptoms of the sickness that, as he used to say later, made him cross the Valley of Death. He was always reluctant to see doctors — he would not tolerate being put into a hospital and being treated as a "thing." Father Weigel neglected himself, and meanwhile the cancer advanced rapidly. Finally, he underwent an operation in April of 1954. The sick man hovered between life and death. A second operation was necessary. The struggle remained indecisive and continued for several weeks. He was sure that he was going to die and prepared himself for it. I asked him one day what he had felt during his agony. His answer was: "Absolute confidence in Christ. It didn't even occur to me to go to confession. Besides, I was very curious to see what things were like on the other side." When the situation prolonged itself, a friend told him in jest that they had already opened a grave for him in the Woodstock cemetery but that, since in the meantime another Father had died, the Rector wanted to ask him if he would be so kind as to yield it to this other Father. His answer was typical of his ever-sharp sense of humor: "The proposition seems very unfair to me, but, oh, well, since it's for an old friend, he can have it."

His recuperation was slow. The cancer had been

completely removed, but the sick man was very weak and had to reaccustom himself to the idea of living. Woodstock and the attention of so many friends who visited him made his convalescence easier. Towards the end of 1954 he was able to walk again in the garden, and at the beginning of the following year, he resumed his teaching.

Forefront of Catholic Renewal

The man who always dreamed of having peace to dedicate himself to his classes and conferences, to study and to write, undertook in the last nine years of his life more feverish activity than ever before. He was not one to make great plans. He was fully convinced that Christian greatness does not consist in ambitious castles in the air but rather in fulfilling with peace and joy the humble tasks of every day. But, for him, everyday tasks were dictated by the needs of others. Whenever people came to him with any kind of request, he saw in their approach a task which God was giving him. And God sent him people in great numbers to ask for his services. As the Archbishop of Baltimore pointed out at the requiem Mass: "No priest in America has been better known, particularly in intellectual circles. No one has been in greater demand for courses of lectures, as preacher on special occasions, as retreat master for priests, and, more recently, for non-Catholic ministers."

The years from 1956 to 1963 placed Father Weigel, along with his friend, Fr. John Courtney Murray, in the vanguard of the renewal movement of the Catholic Church in the United States. Noticing the traditional apathy of American Catholicism to the serious problems of today, he began to advocate a more active and open participation on the part of Catholics in the world of the empirical sciences, of art, of philosophy and of theology. He was convinced that the hour had already come for the Church to leave the ghetto in which it had imprisoned itself since the preceding century and to free itself from its intellectual inferiority complex.

These same years found Father Weigel prominent in the ecumenical movement. He realized with all honesty that the movement favoring the union of the Christian churches had received its first impulse from the Protestant camp. But he was persuaded that the hour had come for the Catholic Church to enter fully upon this path. His numerous personal contacts with theologians and heads of Protestant, Orthodox and Jewish faiths made him a person especially suited for this task. In 1957, he was present as an official observer at the Protestant Conference at Oberlin, Ohio. Likewise he participated as official Catholic observer at the Conferences of Rochester and Buck Hill Falls, Pennsylvania.

During this same time, he published several books and numerous articles about the ecumenical movement. *A Catholic Primer of the Ecumenical Movement* (1957), *Faith and Understanding in America* (1959), *American Dialogue* (1960), *Churches of*

North America (1961), and *The Modern God* (1963) were outstanding. The ecumenical dialogue likewise led him to give courses and conferences in the leading Catholic and secular universities of his country. As a result of these activities, various universities — Georgetown, Vermont, Yale, Alfred, St. Mary's College, Catholic University of Chile — felt privileged in bestowing upon him honorary doctorates. The words with which Yale University conferred this distinction upon him are significant: "You have breached the wall of the Reformation and have made a pioneering effort in the Catholic - Protestant dialogue."

It is no wonder, then, that during the preparatory stages of Vatican II, Father Weigel should have been summoned by Cardinal Bea to participate in the work of the Secretariat for Christian Unity. He took an active part in editing the excellent schema prepared by this Secretariat. During the Council, besides his work of briefing the observers of the non-Catholic Churches about the proposals, he would get together with them every day to listen to their suggestions and make sure later that these reached the Council Fathers. In all of this immense labor he was convinced that the union of the Churches is not something that men by their own will and compromise could effect at the moment they desired. He reminded the impatient that the realization they desired would come when and in the way God sees fit. Our task consists in promoting common dialogue and, in the measure that it be possible, conquering the prejudices that separate us, and drawing together with frankness and charity.

His Interior Life

All of this tireless activity sprang from an intense love of the Church. Despite his already known reluctance to appear pious in his classes, conversations and writings, there shone forth his enthusiastic dedication to the service of the Church — the Body of Christ—the People of God—the presence and living sign of the pardon and love of God in this world. Man should not shut himself up in an individualistic pseudo-mysticism which pretends to deal alone with his God, but he must seek the Infinite in the Church. And he loved the Church as it is, as it presents itself to us today with its greatnesses and miseries, with its enervating sluggishness and its ever-new and transforming message. To those who rebelled at seeing stains and sins in the Church he taught patience to accept it as it was and not to be scandalized. "If it is good enough for God, it should be good enough for me," he would say wisely, with one of his habitual understatements. In this way, he would counteract the pharisaic attitude of the man who leaves the Church because he sees defects in it.

His life as a Christian was also marked by a profound humility. In this he was openly recognized as a spiritual son of St. Augustine, whom he admired immensely. Humility made him wait for all things from the divine grace without ever placing his confidence in his own strength. He seemed to enjoy not hiding his own defects, hoping that grace would overcome them. Not that he accepted a "mysticism of sin," but he did believe that it is in human weakness that the strength of Christ's grace manifests itself.

His humility was likewise manifest in his unwillingness to plan ambitiously his own course of life, but rather in awaiting from God — who speaks through the concrete circumstances of every day — the direction of the path he should take. The saying of Dante, "In His will is our peace," gave him great strength. This will he saw expressed especially in the concrete demands of charity, in not leaving unanswered the thousands of requests of those who came to him in search of instruction, orientation, consolation or simply a moment of friendship. He conceived of the priesthood basically as the service of others, and he surrendered himself completely to that service of others.

This brings us to the deepest part of Father Weigel, to that which cannot be forgotten: his large, wide heart, his friendship open to all. Without pose and without fuss — almost disguising his affection behind a forbidding exterior — he enjoyed forgetting about himself and giving himself to others. Giving himself in matters great and small, concerned with both the greatest need of his friends and the insignificent detail.

Giving himself to all: to the poor and to the rich,

to believers and to unbelievers, to grownups and to children, to his countrymen and to foreigners. This is why those who were his students and those who drew near to him with their problems will never forget him; and this is why, after more than ten years, a beggar-woman of the streets of Santiago whom he had helped kept writing to him. This is why he will not be forgotten by the children whose confessions he had heard and with whom he had played during the summer courses at Fordham University, by the chauffeur of the Baltimore-Woodstock bus, and by Luigi, the Italian youngster to whom he had taught English in the midst of the bustle of the Council. This is why we Chileans preserve his name as a synonym for "loyal friend."

Death

Death found him in the midst of his work. He was tired during the Council. He used to work from 5:30 in the morning till late at night. Nevertheless, he always found time to perform small services for the observers of the other Christian Chuches and for his acquaintances. When he said goodbye in December, he spoke to me of how happy he was at the thought of being in Woodstock that afternoon. He hoped to have some months of peace to give to teaching (he loved to teach!), to read, to write something really worthwhile, but peace did not come. Bishops, students, nuns, Protestants, Jews and Catholics from every social and intellectual walk of life began to shower him with every kind of request. His secretary tried to refuse the invitations, but Father Weigel never refused when someone reached him personally.

His last trip to New York was not recorded in the engagement book kept by his secretary. He went there one night to speak on the following morning at an ecumenical meeting of Jewish rabbis. He stayed at Campion House, the Jesuit residence of *America* magazine. Upon returning from the conference at midday, he said that he did not feel well and that he would not go to lunch. He went to his room and there suffered a double heart-attack. He was found a few minutes after his death, and immediately given the last sacraments. Father Weigel had always been impressed by the fact that St. Ignatius Loyola had died alone in his room in Rome.

His funeral was an impressive epitome of all that he had lived for: the Archbishop of Baltimore celebrated the Mass and gave a brief funeral oration; Chile was represented by the wife of our Ambassador in Washington and by two Jesuits from Chile who served the Mass; the Woodstock choir sang the hymn of Martin Luther, "A Mighty Fortress Is Our God"; at the Offering the litany of the Byzantine Liturgy of Russia was sung; eminent representatives of the Orthodox, Protestant and Jewish faiths were present and raised to God a prayer of thanksgiving for their friend.

AN UNCOMMON ECUMENIST

by ALBERT C. OUTLER

My first "discovery" of Father Weigel was fifteen year ago, when I chanced upon an article of his, in *Theological Studies* (1950), on "Protestant Theological Positions Today." His appraisal of those "positions" was finally negative but he had obviously read an immense swatch of Protestant theology widely and perceptively, and this was a new thing among the Roman Catholics I had known. It was an intriguing phenomenon — a theological conservative and an ecumenical pioneer. Here was a man who stoutly defended *Humani Generis* (in another *Theological Studies* article, in '51) and yet was himself involved in frank and open encounter with the critical spirit condemned by Pius XII — an encounter bound to generate serious tensions in Catholic thought and pose novel challenges to Protestantism. Here was

Catholic ecumenism without a whiff of "indifferent-ism," but with no "immobilism," either.

The chance to get acquainted with so uncommon an ecumenist came at the first North American Conference on Faith and Order at Oberlin in 1957, where he and Father John Sheerin were unofficial Catholic "observers." They were remarkably easy to get to know, wonderfully interesting to talk to. Oberlin was Weigel's first prolonged exposure to Protestant churchmen assembled and he was frankly baffled by their ease with themselves in the absence of any common or visible *magisterium*. But he had the rare gift for listening — really listening! Dialogue was no parlor sport for him but rather a vital business in which speaking the truth in love was the only rule that mattered.

It was nearly six years later (April, 1963) that we met again, at Princeton Theological Seminary, at a conference of psychiatrists, psychologists and theologians on "Will and Willing." Once we had demonstrated that this inescapable problem was also insoluble on any terms available to us, the discussion turned out quite profitably. It was assumed, naturally, that Father Weigel's role there was to expound and defend the Thomist views of freedom and responsibility. Actually, his liveliest contribution was a nimble refereeing of a brisk exchange between Professor Edward Dowey and me — a version of Calvinist determinism vs. a Greek patristic notion of freedom as ingredient in self-consciousness. My dominant memory from those days, however, is of this black-cassocked son of Ignatius mingling so casually with that motley crew of doctors and professors — neither aggressive nor defensive, asking and being offered nothing more than argument and evidence. It was a useful object lesson.

By then, of course, the first session of Vatican II had come and gone, and Pope John lay dying. Though already appointed an official observer, I had passed up Session One because the preparatory reports had been so discouraging that it seemed plain that there were other things more pressing on my calendar! So Father Weigel took the time to brief me on what I'd missed and to prophesy a bit about Session Two — if and when the new pope (but who?) reconvened it.

Our next reunion came in Rome the following September. He was one of the "interpreters" supplied us observers by the Secretariat for Promoting Christian Unity — a desperate need, for the whole experience invariably began by being practically incomprehensible to every newcomer. Father Weigel took a few of us under his wing and taught us first the rudiments and then the finer points of the art of Council-watching. St. Peter's is a triumph of baroque art and architecture, the Vatican a persistent aggregate of baroque society. But Father Gus was not a baroque man. He had long since disengaged the Catholic tradition, to which he adhered *ex animo*, from its post-Tridentine setting, about which he was openly critical, in a spirit at once compassionate and devastating.

From him I quickly learned to look at the Council bifocally: to see the difficulties and obstacles blocking reform; to appreciate the miracle that was bringing reform about.

Morning after morning, we sat together in the observers' tribune, with Weigel for our supplementary eyes and ears. He translated what was said and explained what was going on. He could identify the *dramatis personae* of the Council and decode their ceremonial rhetoric, which he did with trenchant annotations. He also helped me realize the importance of the Council's *pre*history for any understanding of its unfolding process and so prompted a crash program of frantic reading of 19th and early 20th century Catholic history and theology.

As if this weren't enough, he went further. The crucial business of Session Two was the revision and re-revision of the schemata under debate, and this was hard to follow. So, over and beyond the call of duty, Father Gus arranged an extra half hour each morning, in which he translated the texts up for discussion in the general congregation and answered our questions. We called it "Weigel's Workshop" and it was invaluable. But it took time and energy he didn't have to spare.

For, besides his assorted services to the observers, he was also the star of the American Bishops' Press Panel. Every afternoon, on the *Via della Conciliazione*, a swarm of journalists and visitors jammed a basement room in the USO building to hear a team of crack newsmen quiz a panel of council experts (Sheer-in, Connell, Higgins, McKool *et al.*) on the daily doings in the Council and the Vatican. This was one of the most significant operations in the whole urgent enterprise of getting the council rightly understood and fairly reported. Weigel could always humanize and dramatize Council news and yet also convey a powerful sense of its transcendental significance.

As we so often do with our friends, we supposed that since Father Gus seemed to be surviving this killing pace, he must be indestructible. The only time a worrisome doubt on this point crossed my mind was on the eve of the end of the session. It was at a dinner party at Bishop Gorman's apartment on the Via Montserrato. The company, the food and the talk were all superb, but Father Gus was subdued, as I had not seen him before — listening but not talking much, slumped in one of the deep-cushioned chairs in the *salotto*. But he was back in St. Peter's the next morning, for the closing session, chipper and witty as ever in his comments on the fuss and feathers of the great spectacle, fluent as ever in his translations and commentary. He was pleased with the Pope's proposed pilgrimage to Palestine, unimpressed by most of the rest. His final summary was a typical Weigelian aphorism: "Not good enough, but far better than we deserved!"

Afterwards, in the bright sunlight in the Piazza, we shook hands to part. He quipped something about going back to his work at Woodstock and watching the next session from a more tranquil station. Neither of us guessed then the richer meaning of this light-hearted prophecy. Somehow, though, I felt moved to a heartfelt farewell bidding: "Go with God." He smiled, and suddenly he was my spiritual director. Simply and humbly he said: "But he always goes with me!" Then he trudged off toward the Jesuit generalate and I headed toward my *pensione*. It was our last earthly meeting.

When the news of his sudden death came, six weeks later, I was both desolated and yet curiously comforted. My deepest grief was for the loss of a great man worn out before his time, the wastage of greatly needed gifts and talents, unique and irreplaceable. But my comfort came from the fact that the Council was already on its way to transforming his vision from idea to program — further, indeed, and faster than he had ever expected.

Blessed are they who have had a few great teachers in their lives: men who initiated them into a whole new world of inquiry and discourse and who left them so oriented that they could carry on thereafter, more or less on their own. Father Weigel was such a teacher to me. More than any other, he shaped my basic perspective on modern Catholicism and gave me my first real confidence in the promise and prospects of really serious Catholic-Protestant dialogue on the hard-core issues that divide us. He confirmed me in the conviction that indifferentism (on either side) is no valid basis for authentic ecumenism, but that flat intransigence is no better. He taught me to look ahead to some future — and not now predictable — transformation that may be given us as God's gift, in his good time and providence. He left me with a program and an agenda — and thus an abiding sense of his spirit continues to define the work there is for all of us, in this *post*-conciliar epoch.

The marvel, of course, is that there is a multitude of people similarly indebted to this strange unsaintly saint. And this has created among us a sturdy comradeship of gratitude and commission — inspired by one whose still-sounding voice now belongs to

... that choir invisible

Whose music *is* the gladness of the world.

A LIVING EPISTLE

OF CHRIST

by DOUGLAS HORTON

For obvious reasons I associate Father Gustave Weigel with the 13th chapter of I Corinthians. The whole chapter points to him, but some of the phrases in the earlier verses seem to describe him with especially happy accuracy.

He spoke with the tongues of men if not of angels. At the weekly meetings at Vatican II held under the auspices of The Secretariat for Christian Unity, when Catholics, Protestants, Orthodox, Anglicans, men from the East and men from the West, Parthians and Medes and Elamites and the dwellers in Mesopotamia, sat down together to discuss the issues being debated at St. Peter's, his presence was simply invaluable, for he was able to serve as interpreter for the representatives of all the larger language groups of western Europe. It was always a pleasure to walk

with him to or from the basilica, for he had so many
friends in Rome that at a busy time of day he could
hardly cover a hundred feet on the Via della Conciliazione without meeting one or more of them —
and the language between them might be any of half
a dozen which Father Weigel knew in the vernacular
of intimacy.

At the Council itself he was a regularly appointed
interpreter to the observers. We were accustomed to
sit in our tribune in little huddles according to language — Germans around an expert in Latin and
German, French around one in Latin and French,
etc. — and around Father Weigel there was always a
group of Americans, together with other speakers of
English who liked Father Weigel's way of putting
things. It was noticeable that his translations were
always shorter than the original speeches on the
floor: he ruthlessly eliminated irrelevant elements.

Father Weigel was much more than a linguistic
genius. He was an interpreter of men, events, and re-
lationships within the church. This is where he might
be said to have *spoken with the tongue of angels,* for
his knowledge of the church suggested that he had
had the same opportunities to look down on the affairs
of men, especially the men of the council, that angels
are said to enjoy. He would have made a very good
angel of a certain sort — but not an angel of judgment. He never carried a flaming sword with him. He
belonged to the company of the benevolently sophisti-
cated: to us observers he opened the Church of Rome

as a good teacher opens a book to a student, commenting always with accuracy, when necessary with patient severity, and never without appreciation. He would even find a kind word for the most Fundamentalist or chliché-ridden speaker.

He had something of the *gift of prophecy*. When others, on both sides of the line dividing Roman from non-Roman Christianity, were moving in their routine grooves as if the church were to be the same in all its expressions until the end of time, he began to preach new possibilities for Christianity. The followers of Christ had done fairly well in keeping the church holy, Catholic, and apostolic, but as for keeping it one, they had not only allowed it to be broken but in recent generations had slipped into the slough of belief that this is normal and not subject to change. Father Weigel did not accept that formula. He did not know how unity would come, but he wagered all the output of his mind and heart on its coming. The findings of Vatican II on ecumenism were already written on the soul of Father Weigel years before they were promulgated.

Father Weigel was a prophet in both senses of the word: he not only *foretold* truth but he *forthtold* it. It is doubtful if there was any other single person in the United States who spoke so effectively for the need of building better relations between the parts of Christendom. He knew his material, as many would-be prophets in the earlier days of ecumenism did not. In the mind of the church in general at that time ecumenists were strays from Cloud-Cuckoo-Land, but Father Weigel had moved among non-Roman Christians long enough to assemble his facts and marshal them formidably. He did not, however, pretend to more knowledge than he actually possessed: a point of his strength lay in his intellectual modesty. He recognized, for instance, that a person looking at a body of faith from outside cannot understand it as warmly and therefore as truly as a person who is a member of the spiritual household built about that faith. One of his aphorisms might well be borne in the minds of all ecumenical inquirers today: "No Catholic can tell the whole truth about Protestantism, and no Protestant can tell the whole truth about Catholicism." Such a premise as this will keep the debate sober, accurate, and heuristic.

He had the basic qualifications for any prophet — the ability to communicate. There was never the slightest suggestion of what has come to be known as a credibility gap between what he believed and what he said. He put himself with such integrity into his words as to give a new illustration of the truth of the saying that the medium is the message. He was his own declaration: because it was easy to believe in him, belief in what he was saying followed naturally.

I am afraid that St. Paul had nothing to say to his Corinthian friends about one virtue which was inborn in Father Weigel — his sense of humor. This is closely allied, however, to the prophetic consciousness. The prophet has a profound awareness that life has a solid foundation, and so has the man with the faculty of finding amusing the superficialities of life. The person with deep insecurity is notoriously devoid of laughter. Both the prophet and the good-natured man sit light to the surface events of existence. "He that sitteth in the heavens shall laugh"— and he that is his servant upon earth shall laugh with him. At the Council all jests, all bon-mots, seemed to roll eventually into, to be treasured by, the infinitely receptive memory of Father Weigel; and his ability to select from his hoard the inevitable illustration to drive home a point with a glint of humor made him not only a table companion for whom a chair would always be made ready but also a public speaker of singular effectiveness.

Father Weigel, being a delightful member of the human race with the limitations attaching thereto, did not *understand all mysteries and all knowledge,* but his flashing insights made it clear to any companion that he lived in, delighted in, and found the meaning of his own life in mysteries and knowledge. It is probably this phase of him which will be remembered longest. The personality traits which meant subtle pleasure to his contemporaries cannot quite be captured in the *littera scripta quae manet.* The memories of them will pass. His interpretations of experience, personal and ecclesiastical, however, will be read and pondered by people as long as his writings are available.

Of Father Weigel's theology much has already

been written and will be. Historians will recall the name given to the thought of a school in Scotland in the late 18th and early 19th century —the philosophy of common sense. This was a rebellion against cutting ideas loose from life and then over-emphasizing their importance. The basic elements of good philosophy belong not merely to the speculations of the learned but to the "common sense and reason of mankind," said Thomas Reid. I have never heard of a theology of common sense, but if any man ever developed such a thing and held to it, that man was Father Weigel. "The Pope," he observed to a small group of us on one occasion, "is no closer to saving truth and has no more right to it than that pious little woman who sells roast chestnuts on the Piazza Santa Maria in Trastevere." This was in fact a recurring theme of his and gave something of a democratic flavor to all his thinking about the church and its mission. I remember how delighted he was with the final edition of the Constitution on the Sacred Liturgy. This was the first of the Council documents to appoint to perdition that caricature of the doctrine of the church which pictured it as a pyramidal structure having its only direct contact with heaven through its papal apex, all the rest of it having only indirect contact through that apex. In season and out of season Father Weigel made it clear to Catholics and non-Catholics alike that the great sacrament after our Lord himself is the Total Church, which imparts the grace of Christ directly by simple virtue of member-sip, and not by virtue of position in it. In this as in other realms of theology Father Weigel never ceased to check speculation against experience.

He probably would never have said of himself that he *had all faith* as St. Paul puts it, but his friends would never have hesitated to say for him that he had all *saving faith*. Father Weigel had that ultimate mark of the thoroughgoing believer — a sense of being at home in this universe, presided over by the God and Father of our Lord Jesus Christ. He never seemed to be only looking in at life, not quite accustomed to it: he was at home. It was his Father's world, in process of being redeemed through the church of Jesus Christ. This does not mean that he took rest in complacency, that "particular smoke in God's nostrils." He rested upon the will of Christ, a living thing, not at all complacent. He once remarked to me that we were divided into different Christian groups by our own opinions about our Lord, but that when we simply lived with him as saints do ordinarily, the differences tended to vanish.

I know nothing of Father Weigel's financial affairs, but it was clear to all who knew him that he had *bestowed all his goods to feed the poor*. In his vow to poverty he had uprooted from his spirit the deadly motive of acquisitiveness. It is a grateful thought that if all men had the same attitude to property that he had, the viciousness of competition and the cruelties of wars between nations and classes would vanish away over night.

If burning is the combustion of energy, if it is pouring out one's strength like a flame, then Father Weigel may be said literally to have *given his body to be burned*. I know no better way of describing the kind of life he led at the Council than to quote a paragraph from the diary I wrote during his last year there.

"He was the martyr of the Council. . . . Rising every morning to say Mass at six, he would return to the pensione in time for breakfast and then gather about him those who needed help with their Latin in reading the schemata before the Council. At nine he would be at the Council Mass and from then on till the congregation adjourned at half past twelve he would sit in the midst of a small group . . . giving immediate translations. . . . In the afternoon Father Weigel would attend the American press conference. . . . The late afternoons and evenings would be taken up with meetings of the Secretariat, which he served as consultant, or with other meetings of many types. . . . With such a schedule as this it is hardly surprising that his body gave out — but even this, in a way, was as he would have had it, for the machine was worn out, not rusted out, and all for the glory of God and the betterment of men."

It will be recalled that St. Paul regarded all the virtues I have listed from his famous chapter as nothing, simply nothing, without *love*. But in Father Weigel this crowning splendor was never absent. It was this quality in him which originally drew my mind, in thinking of him, to this chapter. He did not vaunt himself, was not puffed up, did not seek his own, was not easily provoked. He was a living epistle of Christ.

ONE OF A KIND

by JOHN B. SHEERIN, C.S.P.

It was in the early 1950s that I first met Father Weigel. Certain Church officials in New York City had condemned a motion picture and this had evoked criticism from a few Catholic scholars, writers and journalists. Father John Middleton, pastor of St. Peter's, Barclay Street, in an attempt to bring about better rapport between the Church officials and their critics, had convened a meeting to discuss the Church's role in public affairs. On hand were a number of Catholic luminaries. Father Gustave Weigel, S.J., was one of those who delivered a paper and I can remember that he had a spirited but genial exchange of views with Jacques Maritain. At the time he was not known as an ecumenist. In fact, if my memory serves me correctly, all that I knew about him at the time was that he had been Dean of the

Faculty at the Catholic University of Chile. I do remember, however, his readiness to face up to knotty problems in Church-State relations and to attempt to solve them without undue concern for conventional solutions usually found in Catholic textbooks.

My first intimate contact with Father "Gus" came in September, 1957. Through the instrumentality of Bishop John Wright of Worcester, Father Weigel and I were selected to attend the North American Faith and Order Conference held September 1-8 at Oberlin College, Oberlin, Ohio. It was sponsored by the World Council of Churches. The World Council officials were most cordial. One evening, for instance, some 25 World Council officials and theologians held an informal dinner in honor of the two Catholic observers. Our presence was considered a dramatic development since Cardinal Stritch had forbidden any Catholics to attend the World Council General Assembly at Evanston, Illinois, in 1954. True, there had been Roman Catholic observers at previous *Faith and Order* meetings on the European continent but the Oberlin meeting was the first occasion on which Catholics had attended an official ecumenical meeting in the United States. Although we had been officially invited by the World Council and our presence was approved by five members of the American hierarchy, it was deemed prudent in those cautious and crucial days that Father and I attend in the role of "unofficial Catholic observers."

I remember Father Weigel as being intensely in-

terested in every moment of the Conference. He was
not a man given to extravagant outbursts of praise
but he did express to me his admiration for the theological depth and evangelical sincerity of several
speakers, notably Robert Calhoun of Yale Divinity
School, who incidentally took a very personal interest
in the Catholic observers. He was not quite as impressed by the form of public prayers used by those
who delivered introductory Invocations. He felt that
these improvised prayers were a bit too theatrical for
his taste and he commented that they make one realize the beauty and dignity of liturgical prayer. This
strikes me now as somewhat amusing as Father Weigel was no liturgist and gladly disowned any aspira-
tions in that quarter.

I remember also his appreciation of the courage of
the prelates from the Orthodox Churches who were
very much in the minority but who did not hesitate
to voice their opposition to Protestant opinions about
the Apostolic Succession. He summarized their role
to me one day in football jargon: "These Orthodox
are running interference for the Catholic position."

In accordance with the Holy Office *Instruction* of
1949 we did not attend the formal religious services
held each morning at the Conference. Instead we offered mass each morning at the local parish church,
the Sacred Heart, whose pastor was Father Martin
Engelhardt. One of the words most frequently heard
at the Conference was *koinonia* (fellowship). Usually Father Weigel would rise in the mornings before I

did and he would knock on the door of my room and call out: "Happy koinonia!" After the daily sessions had finished, he and I would go down to the local rectory in the evening to enjoy the generous hospitality provided by Father Engelhardt. There Father Weigel usually inaugurated a discussion of the day's developments but before long, his conversation became a hilarious succession of stories, jokes and banter.

It is interesting now to look back and recall Father Weigel's assessment of the ecumenical developments at Oberlin. (He attended Section II of Division I which dealt with "Doctrinal Consensus and Conflict" while I attended Sec. I, Division I which discussed "Imperatives and Motivations to Unity.") He delivered a talk at St. Mary's Seminary, Baltimore (cf. the seminary journal *The Voice*, January, 1958) in which he said that the tone of the Conference was pragmatic. "This pragmatic point of view, so prominent in the Protestant churches of this country, became stronger and stronger, and by the end of the Conference it became dominant. The test for anything is not its truth but its pragmatic consequences, its efficiency for service and witness. That was the final tone of Oberlin."

I do remember vividly one of the talks, that delivered by John Mackay of Princeton, as tending in the direction of sheer pragmatism. He claimed that the function of the Church is to render service, that the matter of creed should therefore not be stressed as the important thing was to bear witness and do good to all men. At the time, the talk did seem to assume a very cavalier attitude toward doctrine but I wonder if we might look on it in a different light today. The dogmatic *Constitution on the Church* and the pastoral *Constitution on the Church in the Modern World* as approved by the Second Vatican Council, both put a heavy stress on the Church as *servant.*

Oberlin, nevertheless, represented progress — according to Father Weigel. He said that most earlier Protestants, except the liberals, had thought of the Church in terms of an invisible Church. At Oberlin he saw a definite trend toward acceptance of the concept of the Church as a *visible* Church with definite characteristics, i.e. one, holy, catholic and apostolic. In fact, Dr. Calhoun's theme was precisely this, that the Church of Christ is one, holy, catholic and apostolic. Father Weigel felt that it was unclear at Oberlin where the Protestants were going but he said it was clear what they were leaving. Impressed by the sincerity of the delegates in their desire for a visible Church of Christ, he sensed that many of them excluded in advance any possibility of ever uniting with the Roman Catholic Church. He claimed that they saw in the Roman Church a monolithic uniformity that would exclude the broad latitude in faith and the variety in organization they desired. He therefore envisioned an ecumenical impasse: the Protestants would not come to us and we could not in conscience surrender essential beliefs in order to join with them.

Father Weigel always had a profound contempt for belligerent apologetics. He claimed that such apologetics only prevent Protestants from seeing the Church as she is. He deprecated any notion that converts can be made by polemics, insisting that only the God of love and mercy can win men by his grace. He harbored no fond illusions of an attainment of Christian Unity in the immediate future, contending that no one in the ecumenical movement desires unity by compromise for one cannot compromise with the will of God. Nor would comprehension be the answer. By comprehension he meant acceptance of certain principles of faith, polity and worship with certain allowances for variety in understanding those principles and in formulating and expressing them. Comprehension, he said, is congenial to the Anglo-Saxon mind but he saw no possibility that the Roman Catholics and the Orthodox would ever accept it. They insist on a uniform interpretation of ancient creeds such as those of Nicea and Chalcedon.

The entire ecumenical scene has changed radically since the end of the Council. We are now holding formal meetings between official Catholic and Protestant groups here and in Europe, but Father Weigel saw no value in such meetings in view of the prevailing tensions between Catholics and Protestants. In an article in *Thought,* XXX, 1955, he said that an official Catholic delegate to World Council meetings would feel like a misfit because his presence would be a silent protest to all that was going on at the meetings. He thought that it would be a torturing experience for a Catholic to be actively present "in a religious fellowship where the operating postulates of the vast majority convict such belief as archaic nonsense or arrogant blasphemy. If he has to speak to the group he will be misunderstood no matter what he says" (p. 183). The situation had not changed much by 1959. In the June 8, 1959 issue of *Christianity and Crisis* there was an article by Father Weigel entitled "Inside Roman Catholicism" in which he said that American Catholics know little about Protestantism and show no desire to know about it. Was he wrong in his observations? I don't think so. In the same issue of the magazine, William Clancy agreed with Reinhold Niebuhr's statement: "The relations between Catholics and Protestants in this country are a scandal and an offense against Christian charity." Precisely because of the dour climate of Catholic-Protestant relations, Father Weigel felt that informal, unofficial meetings should take priority over official ecumenical gatherings. He felt that charity was the imminent need and that it would be helpful to have small Catholic-Protestant groups get together to speak their minds and hearts freely but with Christian love. The radically different atmosphere today simply calls attention to the colossal obstacles encountered by Father Weigel in his pioneering work as an American ecumenist.

Father "Gus" was, I believe, temperamentally pessimistic. He could nevertheless chuckle over his forebodings when they proved to be unfounded. (How often humor and pessimism are allied, as in the case of Ronald Knox and Mark Twain.) One night, shortly before the beginning of the Second Vatican Council, I accompanied several Paulist confreres to a dialogue at the Church of the Heavenly Rest in New York City, where Father Weigel delivered an address and participated in the dialogue. Afterwards, my Paulist confreres and I invited Father "Gus" to a restaurant for a midnight snack and I asked him how he felt about the approaching Council. He was anything but optimistic, and contented himself with the hope that it would not be a complete catastrophe for the Church. He had been jolted by Pope John's reactionary *Veterum Sapientiae* (ordering that classes in Latin be taught in all seminaries), and by the ultraconservative Synod of Rome over which the Pope presided and by the Holy Office's *monitum* against reading Teilhard de Chardin. Father Weigel feared that these developments indicated that Pope John would be unable to stand up under pressure from the Curia. After the first session had ended, however, his appreciation of Pope John had changed enormously. I was on a program with him at the Dominican College in Washington after the first session and I was happy to hear him laud Pope John to the skies.

Many Americans came to know Father Weigel during the Council as the "star" of the American Bishops Press Panel. This was a panel of eight priests appointed by the American bishops to help the press in the work of reporting on the Council. Father Weigel and I were among the eight. Every weekday afternoon from 3 P.M. to 4 P.M., the panel sat behind a ping-pong table in the basement of the USO office on Via Conciliazione, the main avenue in front of St. Peter's. The correspondents faced us and fired questions about the developments at the Council that morning. Frequently bishops and Protestant observers would attend the panel sessions. Naturally there were occasions on which a panelist's remarks were questioned by a correspondent or bishop but I never remember anyone challenging Father Weigel at any time during the two sessions in which he was a panelist. One afternoon, he responded to a question about Catholic teaching on Church-State relations and the next morning an Italian daily paper published a grave distortion of his remarks. Father Edward Heston, then moderator of the panel, that afternoon deplored the inaccurate reporting in a few remarks to the press. The reporter involved thereupon stood up and insisted that he had quoted Father Weigel accurately. Father "Gus" himself was absent that afternoon but the other reporters defended him and agreed that he had been badly misquoted.

During the second session I became moderator of the panel and saw Father Weigel even more frequently than during the first session. It was obvious to his friends that he was not feeling well but he persisted in working like a Trojan, translating for the observers at the morning session of the Council, handling the crossfire of questions from the press in the afternoon, delivering lectures to national hierarchies or meeting with bishops in the evenings. He was anxious to make the observers feel completely at home outside as well as inside St. Peter's and so he gave them hours of his time. I remember meeting him one day in the square in front of St. Peter's. He had just left the basilica, the morning session having ended, and he was accompanying Bishop Fred Corson, a Council observer, presumably to lunch. Seeing me, Father Weigel waved me over and introduced me to the bishop. I saw a patch of red under the Bishop's collar but I did not hear his name distinctly. So I attempted to kiss his ring but Father Weigel boomed out in amusement: "No, you don't do that to a Methodist bishop." I understand Bishop Corson was delighted with this case of mistaken identity and told the folks back home all about it.

Bob Kaiser, correspondent for *Time,* held Sunday night receptions at his home during the first two sessions and Father Weigel was usually on hand. Many of the American luminaries of the Council were present and it was an unforgettable experience to listen to discussions in which men like Father Weigel, Father John Courtney Murray, Father Fred McManus, Tom Stransky, Gregory Baum and Hans Kung were expressing their opinions. The strain of so many meetings, so many conversations, so many lectures finally began to show on Father Weigel. In the afternoons after the panel sessions, I frequently went with him to the American Bar across the street from the USO. (The American Bar was not an American bar: it served no strong drinks.) Here Father "Gus" had his cup of tea. From his fellow-Jesuits I heard about his stomach troubles and I presume the cup of tea was a "picker-upper." He seemed to shed his weariness at these "tea parties" and his humor was often irrepressible. As a matter of fact, even at his weariest he never fell into the black moods of gloom that descended at times upon other Council "progressives." His pessimism was, I believe, more intellectual than emotional: he saw future problems with painful clarity. This was in contrast to some of the younger *periti* who hit bottom every time the "progressive" cause suffered a setback.

At the press panel the correspondents admired his scholarship but also relished his humor. One day a housewife-correspondent, after Father Weigel had explained the teaching on charisms, proclaimed that she was fascinated by the thought that she could experience a charism as she went about her work in the kitchen. There was a hush for a moment after this unexpected comment but Father Weigel broke the silence with his comment: "Yes, I do think that good cooking is a charism." Sometimes, the humor was at his own expense. One day he was explaining to the press some of the devious ways in which books might be brought under the vigilant scrutiny of the Holy Office. Taking a purely supposititious case, he said: "Let us suppose for instance that someone in Oshkosh wants to report a book." Father Stransky immediately popped up, "It just happens that we have someone from Oshkosh here with us, Bishop Grellinger who lives there at St. Mary's Church." By extraordinary coincidence the Bishop actually was present.

On another occasion, UPI correspondent Lou Cassels asked for an explanation of the difference between a document labelled a Constitution and one classified as a Decree. Father Weigel proceeded to dilate learnedly on various Council documents at great length and he was followed by Father Bernard Haring who also went into scholarly detail in explaining categories of documents. Whereupon Mr. Cassels said that all this reminded him of the story about the little girl who had to write a report on a book on penguins. She said: "This is a book on penguins. This is a very good book on penguins. This tells you a lot about penguins. In fact, this book tells you more than you really need to know about penguins." Another man might have felt deflated but Father Weigel chuckled as much as did the newsmen.

On January 3, 1964 Father Weigel was scheduled to take part in a television program. The organizers of the program phoned that morning about 11 A.M. to say that Father Weigel was ill and unable to participate and they asked me if I would act as his replacement. I had another engagement but a Paulist confrere, Father Norman O'Connor, volunteered to appear on the program, which was to take place later in the afternoon. Then, if my memory serves me correctly, I had a phone call from Father Graham at *America* notifying me that Father Weigel had died suddenly at the *America* house. He had gone to his room on the fifth floor, thinking that he had a gall-bladder attack, but it proved to be a massive heart attack. A visiting Lithuanian priest found him, Father McNaspy anointed him and two other Jesuits did what they could to help but the incomparable Father Weigel was dead. It was a terrible blow for the Jesuits as they had lost another giant, Father LaFarge, only a few months before but it was also an incredible shock and heartache to all of us who had known him. For days the thought of his death almost hanuted me and I found it difficult to believe it was a fact. He was buried a few days later at Woodstock College, Woodstock, Maryland, where he had taught Ecclesiology for many years. Cardinal Shehan offered the mass of requiem and preached the eulogy. Then we left our beloved "Gus" alone with his glory.

The following September the Council opened its third session. Father Weigel's death left a vacancy at the press panel that no other *peritus* could fill. Another familiar face was missing from the ranks of the correspondents, Milton Bracker of the *New York Times*, who had died at Rome after covering the Pope's visit to the Holy Land. The veteran reporter and the beloved Jesuit had been good friends and it was ecumenically appropriate that another friend of both men, Dr. Claud Nelson, a Methodist minister and correspondent for Religious News Service, should propose that all present at the press panel that day offer a silent prayer for the Catholic priest and the Jewish correspondent.

Towards the end of the third session, a number of Council observers expressed a wish to hold a memorial service for the man they had come to know and admire. It was decided that a scriptural service be held at the Foyer Unitas one afternoon after the regular daily meeting of the Council. Unfortunately it turned out to be the worst possible day for such a service for it was, at least for Americans, the darkest day of the whole Council. That morning, as the American bishops waited anxiously to vote in regard to Religious Liberty, Cardinal Tisserant had announced that there would be no vote. Which meant that Religious Liberty would be tabled until the fourth session. Within a few hours, the American bishops had gathered about 1500 signatures protesting Cardinal Tisserant's decision. The atmosphere that afternoon among the Americans was like the atmosphere in American living rooms the day of the attack on Pearl Harbor. Frustration, fear, suspicion, disappointment, anguish brooded over the circles of American bishops, periti and observers who awaited the Pope's decision in painful suspense. Unfortunately, the date for the memorial service could not be postponed and so it was held at Foyer Unitas. The Lutheran observer, Warren Quanbeck, read a passage from Scripture. Father Thomas Stansky, C.S.P., was also to have read from the Scriptures but the furor

over Religious Liberty demanded his presence else-
where. He asked me to take his place and read the
passages which he had selected and I did so. Dr. Albert Outler, Methodist observer, delivered a brief but
eloquent eulogy, full of grateful affection for Father
"Gus." Of the others present at the service, I remember especially Douglas Horton, Bishop Willebrands
of the Secretariat for Unity, and an Oriental observer
who had written a tribute to Father Weigel and pre-
sented it to us in his own handwriting.

Since the end of the Council, I have often found
myself wondering how Father Weigel would have re-
acted to the final Council reforms as approved by the
Bishops. I think he would welcome especially the new
emphasis on the pastoral role of the Church. A scholar himself, he was always ready to give praise to
scholars but he did not take kindly to the ivory tower
type of scholar. He loved the *world*—in the best sense
of that word. He was always at ease with the people
of his time and in admiration of its culture although
he was also keenly conscious of the perversity and
evil in the movements of the time. He had no desire
to flee from the world but to know and love all that
was best in it and he frequently decried the readiness
of certain active religious orders to become monastic.

Father Weigel's death was a great loss for both
Church and world but God's thoughts are not our
thoughts nor His ways our ways and it is futile to try
to understand why the Lord did not give him more
years of life. It is better for us who have had the

unique privilege of his friendship to pray for him, and to thank God for having known a great scholar, a loveable human being and a dedicated priest.

UNSTUCKNESS

by REVEREND HOLT M. JENKINS

In August of 1962 Father Weigel led a Retreat for Christian Clergy at Loyola-on-the-Potomac in Southern Maryland. Although this Retreat was ecumenical and included clergy of many Christian bodies, it was a traditional Retreat. As such it followed The Spiritual Exercises of Saint Ignatius Loyola and Father Weigel showed himself to be an able guide and interpreter of Ignatian spirituality.

I had already met Father Weigel on several occasions and heard him speak about the Ecumenical Movement. I had also read several of his books. But this was my first acquaintance with him as a spiritual director and retreat leader.

In the course of the Retreat Father Weigel introduced a new word into my vocabulary. The word itself and the concept for which it stands summed up the whole retreat experience for me. It has been part of my vocabulary, and I trust, of my life ever since. Father Weigel's word was *unstuck*.

Now all of us know what it means to be stuck. We are stuck in traffic jams and with responsibilities which we would like to avoid. Sometimes we are stuck with possessions or obligations which we don't really want and can't find a way to get rid of easily. We are stuck with many things which no one else seems to want to take off our hands.

We need to know what it means to be unstuck. This is what Father Weigel taught me. This is also, I think, the principle by which he lived and which enabled him to minister to so many different people in so many different ways. It is unfortunately true that spiritual terms so often carry with them the wrong connotation. Traditional language is subject to so much misunderstanding and misinterpretation. This is especially true of the vocabulary of asceticism. Asceticism has been part of the Christian life since the earliest days of the Church. It is a valid and necessary part of Christian vocation and experience. Originally it had to do with the training of an athlete. It made up the discipline, the practice sessions, and the training table rules of athletes. Saint Paul gives us a picture of this in the ninth chapter of First Corinthians.

However, asceticism has been widely confused with Puritanism. Now Father Weigel was not a Puritan. All who ever knew him are aware of that fact. But he was a Christian athlete. (A physical athlete he never was. He hated exercise and physical fitness programs.) He was an ascetic and a teacher of asceticism. His asceticism consisted of being unstuck.

Much of the traditional language of asceticism suggests an unworldly or otherworldly attitude. This is especially true of words like "detachment" and "abandonment." Although it is, it is not the true meaning of these words; they can be and have been misinterpreted and misunderstood. Because of this the truth which these terms attempt to convey has often been rejected by many Christians.

To practice abandonment suggests the cessation of activity, participation and involvement. To be detached seems to mean or is capable of meaning being out of touch. Detachment can even be interpreted as being psychologically withdrawn.

Such words, therefore, often have an appeal to those who find nothing good in this present world. Those to whom there is nothing attractive about pleasure can use these misunderstood terms to condemn the enjoyment of pleasure by other people. The brand of "worldliness" is so easily bestowed and so difficult to deny. If it really is a bad world, then of course it should be abandoned. If life is harsh and ugly and never beautiful or good, detachment suggests a way out.

It is perfectly true that all of us are somewhat ill at ease in this world. We keep hoping for something better. But *it is a good world*. God has said that it was good and he certainly should know. After all, he made it. And for a little while, for a few years, it's the only world we have.

The ugly old heresy that the world is evil and men are good keeps coming back to haunt us. It's so easy to believe that evil demons labelled money and sex and alcohol reach out their arms to encircle and entrap and enslave the innocent. All of us are to some extent conditioned to this way of thinking. The child who bumps into a table spanks the table and says "bad table." But this is very poor theology. It denies both character and responsibility. It seeks to proclaim an innocence which we have lost.

The Gospel says that we are exactly as God made us, defiled by nothing exterior to ourselves, defiled only by the power of sin. The world is certainly "in sin." It is obviously sinful. But we are the ones who imported sin into the world.

The whole question of a Christian asceticism rests squarely upon the fact that sooner or later the problem of reconciling spiritual life with daily life arises for us all. It is simply impossible to have a spiritual life which is entirely separate from newspapers, television, dish washers and washing machines.

We live in the middle of the inconveniences, the hopes, the expectations of a house that is being remodeled or rebuilt. We are that house. Within ourselves and within our lives something is always being torn down and something else is going up in its place. We are part of a never-ending spiritual program of urban renewal.

One doesn't need to look for things to be ascetic about or for ways in which to practice asceticism. It is all given to us in our daily life. We need only to recognize the need. Everything else has been provided.

This is the whole point of what Father Weigel meant by being unstuck. In unstuckness you don't lose touch. There is no separation from the world. Something from which you are unstuck is still there. You just try to keep it from sticking to you the way your clothes do on a hot day. You can't get rid of responsibilities and obligations and material possessions. You just have to keep them from sticking to you. Instead of being stuck, the Christian must learn how to be unstuck.

The world is not sinful except insofar as we who live in the world are sinful. We must continually learn and practice how to use the things of the world, all of the events and circumstances and possessions which are external to ourselves, in ways which will express our love for God. It is the degree of our attachment to them, the extent to which we are stuck to them, which makes all the difference between spiritual freedom and spiritual bondage.

Unstuckness is a matter of balance and equilibrium. It is like walking on the pavement and trying not to step on the cracks.

If we do not withdraw ourselves sufficiently from worldly interests and concerns we end up by being stuck. If we withdraw completely and successfully then we no longer have any worldly circumstances in which to be interested or for which we can accept responsibility. We have only succeeded in taking ourselves right out of the world which God made and in which he became incarnate. No one ever learned that kind of spirituality from Father Weigel.

Christianity for him was never a religion of impoverishment but always one of enrichment. To be with him in any kind of gathering was always to be enriched by his personality and conversation and deep spirituality. His concern for the things of the Spirit, his own very evident quality of unstuckness was right there on the surface for everyone to see. You might not understand it or be able to account for it but you couldn't miss it.

This was the whole basis of the attractiveness of the man. He was able to lay on the table all that is unique in the Christian life without rejecting the world and the things of the world. Father Weigel was a very human man. His humanity was the product of his unstuckness.

A FIGURE IN TRANSITION

by REV. EUGENE BURKE, C.S.P.

"A kind of figure in transition" — so did Father Weigel describe his work one evening in the later fifties while we were driving from Washington to Woodstock. He meant it in a self-deprecatory way. As the conversation made it clear that the real future of theology was well over the horizon, and the real potential lay not with 'our generation' but with the young theologians and the men still in the seminary. His job was to open some doors for them and incite some to go through those doors and open others.

Between the time of that conversation and now we have seen the beginnings of a transforming change in the life of the Church: The Secretariat for Christian Unity, Vatican II, the Constitution on the Church, the Decree on Ecumenism and its affirmation that ecumenism is itself an integral dimension of the mission of the Church. All these serve to give a differ context to his remark and a much more profound meaning. It seems to me Father Weigel was a figure in transition in the sense of a symbol and sign of the transition — a transition which he played no small part in making possible here in the United States. And he was able to do it because he was in its richest Christian sense a man of tradition, a man shaped and permeated by the Christian experience and open to God's Word as He speaks it today.

My own awareness of this goes back to a moment when our acquaintance began to become friendship. It was 1951 and we had been asked to collaborate in presenting papers on the Encyclical *Humani Generis* issued the previous Fall. He suggested that he would like to cover the historical background if I would take up the doctrinal matter. This called for several meetings in the next few months, some of which were quite tense. For while we were both formed in the Scholastic tradition and had taught a good deal of theology in that tradition we differed strongly. I was still dominantly a Denzinger theologian just beginning to acquire a historical consciousness. Father Weigel already had this consciousness with a strong awareness of the contingencies of history and the complex factors that conjoin to create a particular historical moment. In contrast to my tendency to set the problems into clear but abstract categories he emphasized moods and permanent psychological attitudes always present in the history of theology. It was a perspective that has played an ever increasing role in my teaching since. By way of a footnote to this: at the actual meeting a noted physical scientists took sharp objection to a too 'simpliste' categorization that I had; Father Weigel, sensing what I had intended (but not said), responded with grace and humor and saved me and the situation.

The personal relationship that resulted from this experience served to introduce me into the ecumenical concerns that dominated so much of Father Weigel's later life. He had already written articles that had been most illuminating for me — one on Paul Tillich and the other on contemporary Protestant theology. These served as a beginning for me. As Father Weigel became more and more involved as observer or speaker at ecumenical gatherings I became increasingly aware of the ferment and potential in ecumenism. He was well informed on the European element and able to furnish a critical range of sources for someone like myself just beginning to be professionally interested as a theologian.

In the late fifties and early sixties I was on three or four programs with him and participated in a number of informal situations in which Protestant and Catholic clergy met for discussion. Here I think you saw Father Weigel at his best. At a moment when ecumenism was for the Catholic a tentative if not esoteric operation, great care had to be taken by and for Catholics. We had not really spoken with our fellow Christians in centuries. How avoid categories hardened by centuries of polemical connotations without seeming to abandon orthodoxy? How to touch neuralgic nerves, both Protestant and Catholic, yet maintain charity? In all this Father Weigel was the very embodiment of Hemingway's "grace under pressure." Enabling him to do this was a combination of many things that were constitutive of his personality. He had deep desire to understand the real mind of the person he was dealing with, and an almost intuitive acuity in putting his finger on the personal question at issue. Along with this was the strongly conveyed sense of seeking out the answer together or at least realizing together what the real question was. Also notable was a flexible, modern vocabulary that allowed him to be precise yet effective in explaining his position and understanding the other. Finally when the chips were down he had a bluntness that could be singularly gracious and resolved the issue without closing the door.

Perhaps my personal memory of Father Weigel can be summed up by saying he was both a friend and a teacher and became my friend through teaching me. His ability to evoke reaction by statements he knew you would challenge, his willingness to argue at length, his imperturbability in heated debate that he could so often terminate with a roar of laughter — all these were authentic teaching media. But giving them force and warmth and personal impact was the self-giving that made them live.

AN ECUMENICAL PIONEER

by ROBERT McAFEE BROWN

One of my first public appearances with Father Gustave Weigel, S.J., was at St. Peter's College in Jersey City. We were on a program with Will Herberg and the three of us converged somewhere outside the main building. This was one of my first excursions into "the land of the Jesuits," and I recall feeling a bit lonely. We went in the main door, which closed behind us. We went through a door into a long corridor, and as that door closed behind us, various black-robed figures seemed to appear from all directions. We walked down the corridor and into a small room, the door closing behind us and more black-robed figures engulfing us. We finally went into a small inner room, the private office of the Father Rector, and as that door closed a voice was heard to say to Herberg and myself: "I think we'll just line you up against the wall and shoot you right here."

The voice, I discovered a few seconds later, was the voice of a photographer.

There was a time, not too many generations ago, when the *double entendre* wouldn't have eased the tension but only intensified it. As it was, the room was suddenly transformed into a laughing Jew, a laughing Protestant, about a dozen laughing Jesuits, and one embarrassed photographer. And while it will not do to remember Father Weigel as The Laughing Jesuit (for he could be stern on occasion), it is better to remember him thus than in the rather prim manner in which we usually remember the dead. Indeed, it was the mark of real inspiration that, when his friends at Woodstock College sent out a prayer card for Father Weigel after his death, the picture they put on it was a picture of Father Weigel laughing, rather than a picture of Father Weigel the solemn-faced Jesuit theologian. It was the appropriate tribute, and the way to etch a memory of him firmly in his friends' minds.

That must be the way he is remembered — as a great, openhearted man, who by the genuineness of his personal concern for others broke through barriers between Catholics and Protestants, Catholics and Jews, Catholics and secularists. One need not be long-faced, and one need not be sentimental, in remembering him. It would never do, for example, to characterize Father Weigel as a great letter-writer. He was a terrible letter-writer, as he was the first to admit. In all the process of our writing *An American Dialogue* together, I was able to get only one short note out of him, in which, after having read my half of the book he confined himself to suggesting that I move Maria Laach monastery back to Germany where it belonged. But he was a good man on the telephone, and if you wanted a quick response from him, you had to track him down to a phone booth. If you did, you could be pretty sure that his response to your request would be in the affirmative. He was a great man in conversation, giving himself unstintingly to anyone who had a question — as I learned many times during the course of the second session of the Vatican Council.

Americans need to remember that until Roman Catholic ecumenism got off the ground about five years ago, during the pontificate of Pope John, its advance guard tended to be European. We Protestants, describing the ecumenical attitude in Catholocism, would refer to people like Yves Congar, Abbé Couturier, George Tavard, Karl Adam, Gregory Baum, and others. When asked who the ecumenically minded American Catholics were, we would start off enthusiastically, "Well, there's Father Weigel . . ." and then discover, as our voices trailed off, that we had just about exhausted the list of ecumenically minded American Catholics.

The fact that ecumenism has now entered American Catholicism to stay should not blind us to the fact that there were long, lean years when most of it was borne on the broad and capable shoulders of Gustave Weigel, S.J. He was in this arena, working vigorously, long before it was popular or even "safe." (They say that the place where he used to celebrate Mass at Woodstock College was known as "the Protestant chapel.") For years he roamed the length and breadth of the country, talking to this group and that, appearing on innumerable college campuses, speaking in Protestant seminary lecture series, participating in three-faith discussions, and all the rest. Indeed, it is partly, perhaps principally, because he bore this weight so effectively and so unstintingly, making himself available with such staggering generosity of time and energy to non-Catholic groups, that his heart quietly stopped beating early in January, shortly after his return from Rome and the Council.

Those of us who saw him at the Council every day frequently commented on how tired he appeared to be, and he himself was aware that he was worn out. Indeed, he had been to the doctor on the day of his death and had been told that he must get some rest. As I remember his days at the Council, it is a little hard for me to conceive of him as "resting," though he was, toward the end of the session, trying to cut down on his evening engagements.

He would begin each day before 6 a.m., getting up to say Mass, and would appear in the dining hall of our *pensione* promptly at 7 a.m., where I used to meet him and eat with him. At about 8 a.m. he would meet with the English-speaking observers in the lounge of the *pensione* and translate for us the portions of the *schema* that were to be discussed that morning in the

Council — a completely "extra" assignment that he volunteered to do simply to help us out. Then from 9 a.m. until noon he would sit with us in the observers' tribune, translating all the Latin that was being spoken in the Council session — one of the most exhausting intellectual exercises ever devised by man. Every day from 3 to 4 p.m. he would serve on the American press panel, subject to a steady barrage of questions by 70 to 75 newsmen, and as the late Milton Bracker of the New York *Times* commented, he was really the star of the panel, both for his wit and his clarity. (After doing considerable research in the matter I've come to the conclusion that it was Father Weigel who invented the "ecumenical cocktail," a "dry Montini.") On most afternoons he would have a meeting from 4 to 6 or 6:30 p.m., concerned with one or another of the functions of the Council, and there was usually an evening meeting at which he was obliged to be present.

These were only his regular appointments. In addition, there were always the extra demands being made by people who knew he wouldn't turn them down. When I suddenly found out one day that I was due to address the American *periti* the next afternoon on Protestant reactions to the "religious liberty" chapter of the ecumenism *schema*, I instinctively turned to Father Weigel for help in translating it, and he instinctively gave up whatever he was doing that evening, in order to help me.

Indeed, I recall only one way in which he was able

to detach himself from the steady, intensive and relentless pressures of the Council, and he did so in a way that proved conclusively that he was a great theologian. For he indulged in that infallible hallmark of the theological mind — the enjoyment of detective stories. I was the recipient from another of the observers of a fairly steady stream of Agatha Christie and Marjorie Allingham, and I in turn would pass them on to him, and there would be occasional moments of relief from *schemata* and collegiality and married deacons when we would compare the detecting methods of Hercule Poirot and Mr. Campion. Father Weigel particularly liked Mr. Campion because he had a good Jesuit name.

He had the facility of redeeming any moment from undue solemnity that threatened to get ponderous. I recall an afternoon meeting of English-speaking observers and Catholic theologians from the Secretariat for Christian Unity. At the end of the meeting it was proposed that we say the Lord's Prayer together. We observers had been to Mass enough times to realize that the Catholic version of the prayer ends after *Sed libera no a malo* ("But deliver us from evil"). The Catholics knew that our Protestant version includes a final doxology, "For Thine is the Kingdom, and the power and the glory, forever." So, in instinctive gestures to make the other group feel at home, it transpired that on this occasion all the Protestants stopped after "But deliver us from evil," while all the Catholics continued to say the prayer through to the conclusion of the doxology. We commented afterwards on the fact that although it produced a moment of some awkwardness, it was also a rather touching ecumenical gesture. But when I began to get a little starry-eyed about the experience that night at supper, Father Weigel reminded me, "Why shouldn't we Catholics say the final lines? After all, they're nothing but a Catholic addition to the original text."

While I can't be absolutely sure that Father Weigel originated the term "dry Montini," I can be sure that he developed the most helpful categories for distinguishing between the two main points of view at the Council. In the face of the difficulty of contrasts like "liberals" and "reactionaries," or "conservatives" and "progressives," Father Weigel coined the terms "open-door minds" and "closed-door minds." Some of the bishops, he said, were open in their attitude, and some were closed. And the term "open-door mind" turns out to be a good description of Father Weigel himself.

This does not mean that he sat lightly to Catholic dogma or was *avant garde* in his theological opinions. Indeed, he was more conventional and orthodox in his theology than many Protestants were aware, who knew him chiefly through his hearty good spirit and broad humanity. But he did not have a fixed and narrow mind. It was open to new currents, and those who saw him in action at the Council could not doubt that his sympathies lay with the "open-door" fathers who wanted to relate "the faith once delivered to the saints" to the modern world, to the non-Catholic, and to the future — three things feared above all else by the "closed-door" group.

His attitude toward the whole ecumenical problem was constantly enlarging. He said, at one of those early morning breakfast conversations, that in talking with any non-Catholic, he always assumed that the person was somehow within the Church, even though it was difficult to explain theologically how this was so. He and I talked about the possibility of doing a follow-up to our *American Dialogue*. We thought that when the Council had finally adjourned and there had been a chance for Christendom to absorb its insights, it might be time for a new report on the state of ecumenical affairs. I said that I had learned a lot even since the book had first appeared, and suggested that we should each have an initial chapter called *Retractiones* (Retractions), indicating where we had changed our minds about certain things. He was all for this, acknowledging that he too had grown and changed in his estimate of the ecumenical situation, so that what he had written in 1960 was no longer an adequate index of what he thought in 1963.

He was fond of pointing out that being in a religious order was not confining but liberating, and indeed it was his "freedom" as a Jesuit that gave him such maneuverability on the ecumenical scene. And yet he could contemplate what other courses of action might have been like, as on the night he had dinner with our family and remarked a *bit* wistfully as it seemed to me, to our then twelve-year-old Peter: "It would be pretty nice to sit opposite someone like you every meal . . . I wonder what it would have done to my theology."

The ways of Providence are mysterious, and both Catholics and Protestants, confronted with the completely unexpected death of the great-hearted man we all called "Gus," can agree that there was probably no man on either side of the divide we could less afford to spare. To be perfectly blunt, I can think of a good many deaths that would serve to enhance the rapidity of the ecumenical encounter. But Father Weigel was the man we needed just now to help us advance that dialogue, to interpret the Council to Protestants, to explain it to Catholics, to prod those in places of authority to more decisive action. The fact that he is not here to do these things puts a greater pressure than ever on the rest of us. In the past we could count on him to make the overtures, to break through walls of division, to initiate new conversations, but now we will have to do those things with redoubled intensity, that the gains he helped to make are not only consolidated but come to serve as the basis for new breakthroughs.

LIQUIDATOR OF PREJUDICES

by ROBERT BALKAM

Father Weigel's impact on my life has been profound. In fact, even my vocation has been radically changed as a result. In my boyhood as a Massachusetts Congregationalist, a variety of Christian Churches seemed no more significant to me than a variety of magazines — or a variety of colleges. Only Roman Catholic Churches were different and they were strange, sinister, and superstitious.

Through adolescence and the earlier years of my married life, this attitude didn't change. After a period of infrequent church attendance, my wife and I became very interested in The Church of the Saviour in Washintgon, D.C., which described itself as an ecumenical church. The group has no denominational affiliation — but it demonstrated a committed Christianity such as we had never known. As active members, after taking courses in The School of Christian Living, we became very interested in ecumenism. Denominationalism and Roman Catholicism appeared as questions as they never had before. After several years and extensive soul-searching, complicated by a number of emotional roadblocks due to my life-long prejudice, I knew that I would join the Roman Catholic Church, with my wife and our five children.

A month before my profession of faith, at the first Catholic meeting I had ever attended, I heard Father Weigel address the First Friday Club of Washington, D.C. It was January 3, 1958, six years to the day before his death. He described how Protestant-Catholic relations had improved in the last fifty years. He spoke of Protestant trends in the liturgical movement, in the ecumenical movement, and in a new approach to Scriptures. Although I had recently read his "A Catholic Primer on the Ecumenical Movement," it was inconceivable to me that any Catholic should know as much about Protestantism as he did. The fact that he would speak so favorably of Protestant developments in these three areas was even more unbelievable. As he sat down, a priest stepped to the rostrum and admonished those present: "Now don't you men go out and get friendly with those people." I was still one of "those people."

But Father Weigel dissolved many of my prejudices that day. Previously it seemed simply not possible that such a Catholic priest drew breath! From then on I read his books and went to hear him speak whenever I could locate him. Yet, I didn't idolize him. At times I was disappointed. Dr. Robert McAfee Brown's portion of "An American Dialogue" was the better part, I thought. At times I thought he was repetitious. Later I realized that I went to hear him too often at similar meetings. One of my early disappointments emerged later as one more cause for admiration. Whenever he was pressed by a questioner about ultimate Christianity, his reaction was almost like that of a bull to a red bandana. He would reply, almost curtly, that ultimate unity would come only in God's time — "certainly not in our lifetime!" He believed this deeply. He was fully aware of the profound and significant issues which still separate Christians. Burning within him, however, was an even deeper conviction that we must do all we possibly can to bring Christians together — at least for meaningful communication.[1]

His life, certainly the last six years of it, was given selflessly to bringing people together. Competent theologian that he was, a mark of his greatness was his

---

[1] "The ecumenical movement is both an idea and an historical fact. The idea in its abstract purity is simple enough; it is an invitation to the churches professing faith in Jesus Christ to come together in the hope that in some future day they will all be one. The coming together is the immediate goal of the idea. The final union is a desired consequence. It is very important to keep these facets distinct. As so many voices within the historical movement have declared, the final union of the churches must be God's work, exercised in His good time. The coming together is man's work, not indeed without God's grace, yet always with a human appeal to man's action founded on divine trust."

CATHOLIC THEOLOGY IN DIALOGUE p. 69

ready ability to communicate with any person of good will.

In 1960, while making a retreat at Loyola-on-Potomac Retreat House in southern Maryland, I learned that the director, Father James A. Martin, S.J., was conducting annual retreats for Protestants. He invited me to assist him the following year. At the end of the retreat, I said to him: "Father, if you plan to have another retreat next year, the ideal leader would be Father Weigel." "Oh, I know him," he replied, "I'll ask him." By September, 1961, it was settled that Father Weigel would lead a retreat for Protestants at Loyola the following June.

The National Catholic Laymen's Retreat Conference sponsored a retreat for Protestant and Anglican clergymen at Maryland Retreat House, Erlanger, Kentucky, in September, 1961, led by Bishop John J. Wright of Pittsburgh. The press carried a notice prior to the retreat, but I saw no mention afterwards. In November, Bishop Wright spoke in our parish and I mustered the courage to speak to a bishop for the first time in my life. He told me that the retreat had gone very well — nearly forty ministers had participated. I told him of the retreat we planned at Loyola the following June with Father Weigel as leader. Several months later, Father Martin received word that the Retreat Conference wished to sponsor a clergy retreat in 1962 — at Loyola with Father Weigel as leader. Father Martin happily agreed and asked me to help with arrangements.

We started mailing invitations in January, first to those who had made the retreat at Marydale. We wrote to Episcopal and Methodist Bishops, contacted Councils of Churches and Seminary Presidents. The response was most gratifying — and it was before the Vatican Council convened. By late spring we had nearly seventy acceptances and diverted some of the ministers to the June retreat originally planned for laymen only.

In February, I went to Woodstock College, Maryland, where Father Weigel was teaching, to discuss the retreat with him. He met me in the lobby and whisked me up to his room with a flourish, apologized for the half-packed trunks, and seated me on a couch liberally scattered with paperback detective stories. His approach to the retreat seemed casual, yet there was no doubt that he would provide strong leadership.

On the day of the first retreat in June, our 14-year-old son, Cliff, and I drove to Woodstock to pick up Father Weigel. Cliff came along to serve Mass — we were slightly short of Catholics. The ride was a real treat. Father Weigel had an anecdote for nearly every turn in the road — particularly in southern Maryland — which he seemed to know as well as the Ignatian Exercises. We had to stop at the Waldorf Post Office — a mail box wouldn't do — as he had to mail a letter to Rome recommending Father John B. Sheerin, Paulist editor of *The Catholic World*, to take his place at an August World Council of Churches meeting in Paris since he would be leading the clergy retreat at Loyola at that time. In between tales of the Maryland countryside, Father Weigel was regularly inquiring about Cliff's appetite. As we drove into La Plata, he spotted a frozen custard stand and called for a halt. Cliff was all for it, of course. As we went in with great ceremony, Father Weigel confided to me: "I've never tasted the stuff!" We all enjoyed it nevertheless. On the return trip to Woodstock we stopped at another stand west of Baltimore, and from then on, whenever I saw him, he would always inquire for Cliff and say: "Tell him, remember soft ice cream!"

What was the impact of the retreat? An Anglican layman returned and organized week-end retreats at the Washington Cathedral. A South African Pentecostal minister came from his new home in Texas and later went to the Vatican Council. A Lutheran pastor drove from Pittsburgh for the beginning of the retreat Friday evening, but had to leave after dinner on Saturday to return for services on Sunday morning in his own church. Two Anglicans from Philadelphia did the same. Typical comments were: "He rooted the meditations in that which is common to all Christianity — the Lordship of Christ." "One of the finest religious experiences of my life." ". . . This was a rich experience, one not intended to make us Christian Catholics, but one which succeeded, I hope, in making us more catholic Christians."

With nearly a dozen last-minute cancellations due to illness, death, and other pastoral demands, forty-nine clergymen gathered for the August retreat. They came from Chicago and Birmingham, Durham and New York. Reading at meals was from Father Hans Kung's *The Council, Reform, and Reunion*. This was still far out for most Catholic ears — it dumbfounded many of the Anglicans and Protestants. Father Weigel threw himself into the retreat with great intensity. He read from the New English Bible — "It's my favorite — because it's the newest I've found, I guess." His meditations followed the Spiritual Exercises of St. Ignatius. He gave due notice to the First Principle and Foundation — but it was all done with real "Weigelese." Detachment from worldly things as recommended by St. Ignatius became "unstuckness" — certainly it is a description that sticks with you. Asked in a discussion period how he fared with the hierarchy, he said: "Oh, there are some dioceses where I am not welcome. If I were travelling through them on a train and it broke down, I don't know what I would do."

Before celebrating Mass, he brought the vestments out onto the altar and described each one as he put it on. He asked me to read the entire English text of the Mass. The second day, the clergymen asked to make the responses (Latin at that time) and the participation was quite good.

Father Weigel's meditation on the animal sacrifices of Old Testament times as a pre-figuring of Christ's Sacrifice on Calvary was as graphic a word picture from history as I have ever heard. The atmosphere of the chapel was alive with unity between leader and congregation. Between meditations, there was always a line at his door. Two discussion periods were tense and emotion-laden — not with conflict between separated Christians — but with heart-felt questions and statements springing from those whose souls had been deeply moved. Everyone certainly became aware at a deeper level of the unity, albeit imperfect, which already binds Christians together. The pain of remaining barriers was also felt more keenly than before.

As we drove away from Loyola on our return to Woodstock, it was obvious that Father Weigel was totally spent — but it didn't affect his spirit. On the contrary, the self-giving seemed to lift his feelings. In a few miles, Cliff and I were rolling with laughter as he gave the most hilarious and impersonal account of his bout with cancer of the intestine some ten years before — how he twice nearly died (his grave had been chosen at Woodstock) — and ended the narration with an almost casual question: "The Lord saved me then, why shouldn't I give my life now?"

After that I heard him speak four or five times and spoke with him briefly each time — until one Saturday morning Cliff came back from his paper route with the news: "Father Weigel is dead!" As Louis Cassels, religion editor of United Press International and close friend, observed: "It wasn't really unexpected, but it was no less a shock." For me, the shock was accompanied by the question: "How many will it take to replace him?" It was obvious that no single person could fill the gaping void left by his death. Certainly I was probably least of all equipped intellectually to pull any of the load. The heart-rending realization that he *had* died, however, left me with an awareness of some vague call to fulfill part of what he had left undone — and somehow in his spirit. I had no idea of what I might do. It was more than eighteen months before the slightest hint appeared. During that time, after the eulogies appeared, his name seemed to disappear from notice as if he had been quickly forgottn.

Retreats for Fellow Christian Clergymen were held each year at Loyola-on-Potomac. The 1963 retreat was led by Bishop William G. Connare of Greensburg, Pennsylvania. Father Avery Dulles, S.J., was leader of the 1964 retreat. In 1965, it occurred to us to invite Catholic priests to join their Fellow Christian Clergymen .Five accepted and I believe that the impact of the retreat led by Father David Bowman, S.J., was as great on them as it was on the Anglicans and Protestants. During the closing discussion, Monsignor Joseph Denges, pastor of St. Stephen's Roman Catholic Church in Washington, invited the ministers and their wives to a Bible Service and Social Hour at his church in October. This pleased me very much, as we had never had any continuity in the past. Ministers had come from Dallas and Chicago, Birmingham and Detroit. There was a deep sharing for two days — then the farewells came.

Monsignor Denges' invitation seemed an excellent

opportunity to keep the group loosely in contact throughout the year — why not call it "The Gustave Weigel Society"? I discussed this idea with Father Dulles and later with Father John Courtney Murray. They agreed that it might have possibilities. Father Dulles promised to write Father Weigel's sister of our plans.

It seemed appropriate to invite people who had been associated with Father Weigel in ecumenism to be members of a Board of Consultors of the Society. The thought occurred that the one time and place where many of these people would be together would be at the Vatican Council, which was just about to convene for its fourth session. For two months, my wife and I talked longingly of the possibility of going to Rome. As we have eight children, a trip abroad had always seemed out of the question, but this opportunity was too good to miss. In mid-October we were on our way — a pilgrimage by jet to Vatican II.

We had eight glorious days in Rome and found much enthusiasm for the idea. Father John Courtney Murray, in Salvator Mundi Hospital with a collapsed lung, gave us a particularly warm welcome. He readily agreed to be one of the Honorary Co-Chairmen. Bishop Connare kindly obtained tickets for us to the Mass celebrated just before the deliberative sessions of the Council, to a Beatification Ceremony, and to a general audience with the Pope. It was only after we found our seats in St. Peter's that we discovered we were included in a group of about fifty which was taken to a side chapel after the audience and were introduced to Pope Paul individually. It was a thrilling experience!

Mr. Martin H. Work, lay auditor, and Executive Director of the National Council of Catholic Men, introduced me to Dr. Albert C. Outler, Methodist Observer. "May I please be a part of The Gustave Weigel Society? You should talk with Dr. Theodore Mosconas — he and I gave eulogies to Father Gus at the Observers' Memorial Service last fall." Dr. Mosconas has celebrated his twenty-fifth anniversary as librarian of the Greek Orthodox Patriarchate Library in Alexandria, Egypt. My wife and I found him to be a delightful person and he was pleased to be a consultor. Father Thomas Stransky, American Paulist and staff member of the Vatican Secretariat for Promoting Christian Unity, was at first concerned lest we would duplicate the activities of diocesan ecumenical commissions. We pointed out that the Society would aim to bring Christians of various communions together for significant experiences so that they would return to their own parishes or institutions to do the *real* work of ecumenism. After that he was pleased to be a member of the Board of Consultors. Dr. Douglas Horton was about to leave for Athens during the Council recess, but he promised to discuss the Society with Father Murray on his return. He later accepted the position of Honorary Co-Chairman and has exhibited great interest in our activities. We had a pleasant visit with Dr. Douglas Steere at Foyer Unitas where he and Mrs. Steere were staying. He was very much in favor of honoring Father Weigel's memory and pioneering work in this manner. Father John Sheerin, Paulist Father and editor of *The Catholic World,* had been active with Father Weigel from the early days of American Catholic participation in ecumenism. He felt that thus far no one had given proper acknowledgment to Father Weigel's trail blazing. Dr. Robert McAfee Brown, Presbyterian who had co-authored "An American Dialogue" with Father Weigel, was not in Rome while we were there, but he wrote from Stanford that he would be pleased to share the chairmanship of the Board of Consultors with Father Sheerin. And there were others — Dr. Peter Day, Ecumenical Officer of the Episcopal Church in the U. S.; Dr. Robert C. Dodds, Faith and Order Department of the National Council of Churches; Professor Ralph Hyslop, Union Theological Seminary, New York; Father Avery Dulles, Father David J. Bowman, Martin Work, and later Dr. George Lindbeck, Lutheran lay theologian at Yale Divinity School; Professor Warren Quanbeck, Lutheran Theological Seminary, St. Paul, Minnesota; Mrs. Theodore Wedel, Division of Christian Unity, National Council of Churches; and Very Rev. Alexander Schmemann, Dean of St. Vladimir's Orthodox Theological Seminary.

The Bible Service and Social Hour at St. Stephen's took place just three days after our return from Rome, with brief stopovers in Paris and London. When we announced our intention to form the Society, there was general interest, but not great enthusiasm, I thought. Perhaps almost anything would have been anti-climactic to me at that point. Early in the evening, Father James Richards, rector of St. Paul's Episcopal Church in Washington, had offered the hospitality of his church if the group wanted to meet again. After the announcement, I boldly asked him if we could set a date then. He graciously made the invitation specific for the evening of February 15, 1966 — and that became the charter meeting of the Society.

It was a great evening. There were over eighty there, clergy and laity from a broad representation of denominations. Sister Mary Jeremy of the Sisters of Mercy and Father Weigel's niece came over from Baltimore and read the statement of purpose. Three members of the Board of Directors (the governing body, mostly from the Washington area) spoke on the opportunity of The Gustave Weigel Society. The meeting closed with a selection from the prayer service of the Taize Community, led by a Jesuit priest and a Lutheran pastor. The spontaneous prayers were particularly moving.

In April, Louis Cassels spoke on "The Heritage of Father Weigel" at the First Congregational Church in Washington and moved us near to hysterics and tears. A laywoman, a Quaker, and a Benedictine abbot spoke to us on prayer at a meeting at Trinity College in June. Pastor Max Lackmann, German Lutheran, spoke at a meeting at Wesley Theological

Seminary in September and the Rt. Rev. Angus Dun, retired Episcopal Bishop of Washington, addressed a meeting a Dunbarton College in January, 1967 to a group of more than 300.

The Society sponsored three retreats in 1966, including one led by Father Sheerin for ministers and their wives, priests, and religious. Four retreats are planned for 1967, a fitting observance of the 450th Anniversary of the Reformation and a report of the plenary session of COCU by its chairman and a member of our Board of Directors, Rev. David G. Colwell.

Over 280 members from twenty-one states and the District of Columbia, representing an area which extends from Florida to Hawaii, are included in the Society. The membership is about evenly divided between clergy and laity. Nearly half are Anglican, Orthodox, or Protestant.

Gustave Weigel was many things to many people. Some of his students at Woodstock have said he rarely mentioned his ecumenical activities in class. Most non-Catholics thought of him *only* as an ecumenist. Some Catholics judged him to be a pioneer — even a prophet — others feared he was "compromising the faith." Yet, he rested on solid rock. As mentioned previously, he sounded ultra-conservative when pressed on the subject of organic unity. In my judgment he seemed to embody an excellent balance of the exercise of freedom with sincere loyalty to authority — a balance which Catholics and Protestants, believers and non-believers, states and citizens, parents and children all over the world are frantically searching to achieve today. He lived not so many years ago, but life has accelerated even in the interval since his death, and perhaps the ability to live in the midst of the tensions between Protestants and Catholics, between freedom and authority was the greatest message that he left for us. For if, indeed, by the grace of God, we can live in the midst of the tensions which seem to swirl increasingly about us, we will let our lives show to the world the "peace which passeth all understanding."